HANNIBAL

HANNIBAL

Rome's Greatest Enemy

PHILIP FREEMAN

PEGASUS BOOKS
NEW YORK LONDON

HANNIBAL

Pegasus Books, Ltd.
148 West 37th Street, 13th Floor
New York, NY 10018

Copyright © 2022 by Philip Freeman

First Pegasus Books paperback edition January 2023
First Pegasus Books cloth edition February 2022

Interior design by Maria Fernandez

Library of Congress Cataloging-in-Publication Data is available.

ISBN: 978-1-63936-365-0

10 9 8 7 6 5 4 3 2

Printed in the United States of America
Distributed by Simon & Schuster
www.pegasusbooks.com

CONTENTS

Prologue: The Vow   ix

Timeline   xv

Glossary of Names   xix

1 Carthage   1

2 Sicily   11

3 Spain   21

4 New Carthage   31

5 Saguntum   39

6 Gaul   49

7 The Alps   59

8 The Ticinus River   67

9 Trebia   79

10 The Arno Marshes   87

11 Lake Trasimene   95

12 Campania   105

13 Geronium   117

14 Cannae   125

15 Rome   135

16 Capua   141

17 Metaurus   153

18 Zama   165

19 Exile   177

20 Legacy   185

    Epilogue: What If Hannibal Had Won?   189

    Ancient Sources   197

    Modern Sources   201

    Endnotes   205

    Index   211

HANNIBAL

THE VOW

The young African boy and his father walked up the cold stone steps of the temple in the hour just before dawn. The light rising from behind the distant mountains to the east beyond the wide bay was just beginning to spread across the city. He was only nine years old, but the boy had lived here all of his short life and knew every street and back alley. He had wandered every day from the pottery kilns and metalworking quarters on the edge of the massive city walls to the enormous central marketplace beneath the hill called Byrsa where merchants sold beautifully decorated Celtic daggers, necklaces of Baltic amber, Spanish silver, painted ostrich eggs from across the desert to the south, sweet Egyptian dates, Indian spices, the best Arabian frankincense, and even silk from distant China—all the treasures of the known world which flowed endlessly into the great port of Carthage.

His father, Hamilcar of the Barca clan, was the greatest general Carthage had ever produced, but the politicians and wealthy merchant families who controlled the town preferred negotiation and compromise to warfare. Hamilcar had watched in silent rage several years earlier as the Carthaginian *adirim*, or senate, had abandoned the ancient Punic colonies in nearby Sicily to the rising power of Rome. They had even agreed to pay the Romans an enormous indemnity in silver to buy peace. Hamilcar was now on his way to Spain to take over the rich mines of Iberia to help pay the heavy burden imposed on his city by Rome.

The father and his eldest son together entered the cool darkness of the great temple of Ba'al Hammon, chief god of Carthage. Ba'al—the Master or Lord—had come with the first colonists from Phoenician Tyre centuries before when they had sailed to the western Mediterranean in search of new markets and lands to settle. Stories said that Ba'al demanded a *molk*, or gift, of the firstborn child from each family. At the *tophet*, or sacrificial sanctuary, of Carthage near the harbor, the great outstretched metal arms of Ba'al's statue received the child who rolled gently into the flaming pit at its base while the parents watched and the attendants played loud music to cover the infant's screams. In recent years animals had sometimes taken the place of children, though the god could still demand a human victim.

But not today. This was a day for beginnings when Hamilcar would ask the god to favor his efforts across the sea in Spain. It might be years before he returned to Carthage, if ever. The priests sang the sacred prayers in the ancient Punic tongue, then cut the throat of the spotless lamb on the altar so that its blood covered the stone of sacrifice.

When all was done, Hamilcar asked the priests and attendants to withdraw so that he might speak to his son alone. The boy—named Hanniba'al or Hannibal for "he who enjoys the favor of Ba'al"—waited for the others to leave, terrified at what his father might say, or not say. More than anything in the world he wanted to go with him to Spain and learn the arts of war so that he, too, might one day fight for his city. Much to his relief, Hamilcar looked down at his son with a smile on his face and asked the boy in an offhand way if he might like to accompany him across the sea. Hannibal was overjoyed and hugged his father tightly, saying it was his greatest wish.

Then the look on Hamilcar's face changed. In deadly earnestness he told the boy to put his hand on the still-warm body of the lamb on the altar and swear a most solemn oath before Ba'al and all the gods. If Hannibal were to sail with him to Spain to become a soldier for Carthage, he must first vow eternal hatred towards Rome[1], never yielding in his anger and never giving up the fight until his final breath.

Hannibal had been raised since birth on bitter enmity towards the Romans and did not hesitate for a moment to take the vow his father demanded. No matter what the gods held in store for him in the years ahead, he would dedicate his life, his very soul, to fighting against the most powerful and relentless enemy of Carthage.

❦

T he story of Hannibal that began with a young boy in a Carthaginian temple has gripped the imagination of the world for over two thousand years, beginning with the Romans who delighted in seeing the African leader as the embodiment of the supposed barbaric, uncivilized enemies they faced on all sides and whom they longed to conquer. But the fact that Hannibal was one of the most brilliant and daring generals in world history—and the man who almost destroyed Rome—was impossible even for the Romans to ignore. What kind of person would dare to lead his struggling homeland in a war against the most relentless military power the ancient world would ever know? How could he conceive and then actually carry out his audacious plan to march his army over the towering Alps to carry his war into the very heartland of Italy? And how could Hannibal, consistently outnumbered and always deep in enemy territory, defeat Roman army after Roman army that was sent against him until he held the very fate of Rome within his grasp?

Hannibal appeals to many as the ultimate underdog—a Carthaginian David against the Goliath of Rome—but it wasn't just his genius on the battlefield that set him apart. As a boy and then a man, his self-discipline and determination were legendary. As a military leader, like Alexander the Great before him and Julius Caesar after, he understood the hearts of men and had an uncanny ability to read the unseen weaknesses of his enemy. As a commander in war, Hannibal has few equals in history and has long been held as a model of strategic and tactical genius studied in military academies even today. But Hannibal was much more than just a great general. He was a practiced statesman, a skilled diplomat, and a man deeply devoted to his family and country.

Like so many others, I remember as a boy reading with fascination the story of Hannibal leading his battle elephants over the Alps and defeating the unbeatable Romans in a seemingly hopeless war to save his country. But I long wondered: Who was the man behind the legend? What can the stories we have of him—almost all from hostile Roman sources—tell us about the real Hannibal? How does the story change if we look at Hannibal from the Carthaginian and not the Roman point of view? Can we search beneath the accounts of Roman historians like Livy who were eager to portray Hannibal as a monster and find a more human figure? Can we use the life of Hannibal to look at the Romans themselves in an unfamiliar way, not as the noble and benign defenders of civilization familiar from modern history books but as voracious, ruthless conquerors motivated by greed and imperialism?

This biography is my attempt to answer those questions. It is a story of brutal warfare and brilliant military maneuvers on both sides, but even more it is the search for a real person from long ago who stood against the overwhelming power of a mighty empire. It is not the tale of a blameless hero—for Hannibal had faults that would ultimately doom both him and his city—but it is the story of a man who against all odds dared to change the course of history.

TIMELINE

All dates throughout this book are B.C.E. unless otherwise noted.

814	Traditional founding of Carthage
753	Traditional founding of Rome
509	End of Roman monarchy, Roman Republic begins
	First treaty between Carthage and Rome
480	Approximate date of Carthaginian voyages of Himilco to British Isles and Hanno to West Africa
	Syracuse defeats Carthaginian navy at Battle of Himera
390 (or 387)	Gauls sack Rome
348	Second treaty between Carthage and Rome
323	Death of Alexander the Great
310	Agathocles of Syracuse invades North Africa
306	Third treaty between Carthage and Rome
280-275	War of Pyrrhus against Rome

264–241	First Punic War of Rome against Carthage
247	Hannibal is born
241–238	Revolt of mercenaries against Carthage
237	Hamilcar Barca goes to Spain
236	Scipio is born
229	Death of Hamilcar. His son-in-law Hasdrubal takes over command in Spain
226	Ebro treaty between Carthage and Rome
221	Hasdrubal murdered. Hannibal takes command in Spain
219	Siege and capture of Saguntum by Hannibal
218	Rome declares war on Carthage. Second Punic War begins
	Hannibal's marches across the Alps to Italy
	Battle of Ticinus River
	Battle of Trebia River
217	Battle of Lake Trasimene
	Fabius Maximus becomes dictator of Rome
216	Battle of Cannae
	Capua defects to Hannibal
215	Alliance between Hannibal and Philip of Macedonia
	Syracuse becomes ally of Carthage
213	Rome besieges Syracuse
211	Hannibal marches on Rome
	Capua and Syracuse fall to Rome

209	Scipio captures New Carthage
	Rome retakes Tarentum
208	Scipio defeats Hannibal's brother Hasdrubal at Battle of Baecula
207	Hannibal's brother Hasdrubal killed at Battle of Metaurus River
206	Scipio defeats Carthaginians at Battle of Ilipia
204	Scipio invades North Africa
203	Hannibal recalled from Italy to Carthage
202	Battle of Zama. End of Second Punic War
196	Hannibal elected as a chief magistrate of Carthage
195	Hannibal leaves Carthage for exile in the East
184/183	Hannibal commits suicide in Bithynia
	Scipio dies in exile
149	Rome declares war on Carthage and Third Punic War begins
146	Carthage destroyed by Scipio Aemilianus

GLOSSARY OF NAMES

The Carthaginian elite drew on a relatively small pool of names for their children so that it can sometimes be difficult to keep track of who was who. Roman families likewise used the same name generation after generation, so that grandfathers, fathers, and sons are easily confused. This list is a handy reference for readers of the key characters in the life of Hannibal and the larger history of Carthage and Rome.

Fabius Maximus: Appointed dictator of Rome, he successfully waged war against Hannibal by avoiding direct battles, thus gaining the name Cunctator ("Delayer").

Gaius Flaminius: Roman general and foe of the Roman establishment who fell into Hannibal's trap at Lake Trasimene and died there with most of his army.

Gaius Terentius Varro: Roman consul and commanding general against Hannibal at the Battle of Cannae in 216.

Hamilcar Barca: Carthaginian general and father of Hannibal. Commanded Carthaginian troops in Sicily in the First Punic War and subdued much of southern Spain in the years following.

Hannibal: Son of Hamilcar Barca and Carthage's greatest general.

Hanno: Carthaginian explorer who sailed along the Atlantic coast of Africa perhaps as far as modern Sierra Leone.

Hanno: Carthaginian nobleman and politician who was the leading opponent of Hannibal and the Barca family.

Hasdrubal: Younger brother of Hannibal, who left him in command in southern Spain. He marched his army to Italy to aid his brother and died in the Battle of Metaurus.

Mago: Carthaginian general and youngest brother of Hannibal.

Maharbal: Carthaginian cavalry commander, urged Hannibal to march on Rome after the Battle of Cannae.

Masinissa: King of Numidia and ally of Rome.

Polybius: A Greek sent to Rome as a hostage, he became a friend of the Scipio family and wrote the best surviving account of the Second Punic War.

Pyrrhus: King of Epirus who waged war with Rome and invaded Italy.

Scipio: Publius Cornelius Scipio Africanus, general of Rome who defeated Hannibal in the Second Punic War

CARTHAGE

Hannibal's home was founded by a woman—on that everyone could agree.

But cities in the ancient world were never founded by women. Theseus united the villages of Attica to form Athens, King David defeated the Canaanites to establish Jerusalem as the capital of the Jewish kingdom, and Romulus and his brother Remus built the first walls of Rome. The tale of a woman founding Carthage is so odd that it may actually be true, since it isn't the sort of story anyone would invent.

Legend tells[1] how the beautiful queen Elissa fled the Phoenician city of Tyre after her wicked brother Pygmalion murdered her husband. She offered prayers to the god Melqart and sailed with a few followers first to Cyprus, where she rescued eighty virgins destined for prostitution who instead became the wives of her settlers in their new home. When the Tyrians finally arrived in Africa, the native king laughed at the idea of a woman as leader and smugly offered Elissa only as much land for her new city as she could cover with the hide of a single ox. But the clever queen cut an ox hide (Greek *byrsa*) into thin strips and laid them out in an enormous circle around an entire hillside near the coast, thus claiming the citadel—later known as the Byrsa—that would form the heart of her new city. The Phoenician colonists named the town *Qart-Hadasht* ("New City"), which the Greeks would call *Carchedon* and the Romans *Carthago*. Years later, when Elissa's city was well established and a native Libyan king was pressing her to marry him, she died by suicide, throwing herself on a funeral pyre instead of entering into a marriage against her will. Readers of the Roman poet Virgil will recognize the same story, with a few minor changes, told in his *Aeneid* in which the Trojan hero Aeneas visits Carthage and falls in love with the founding queen, named Dido in his poem, who kills herself when he leaves her behind in Africa.

The ancestors of Hannibal[2] did indeed come from the distant shores of the Levant in the eastern Mediterranean Sea. The Greeks called them *Phoinikes* from their word for the valuable purple coloring they extracted from the glands of sea mollusks. This rare dye became the color of kings, but the stench from the factories in which it was made was so overpowering that they were always located on the far edge of town. When the Romans later encountered the Phoenicians, they called them the *Poeni* or *Punici*. They spoke a Semitic language closely related to that of their Hebrew neighbors and were among the first people to develop an alphabet.

The Phoenicians were never a united empire, but instead a collection of independent city-states that included Tyre, Sidon, and Byblos. Often overrun by warring empires and having little in the way of natural resources aside from mollusks and cedar trees in the mountains of Lebanon rising above their cities, the Phoenicians turned to the sea and became the greatest sailors of the ancient world. By the tenth century B.C.E., they were establishing trading posts across the Mediterranean to bring the raw materials of the west to the hungry markets of the east. Cyprus and Sardinia, with their rich deposits of copper, lead, and iron, were among the first places where Tyre and other Phoenician cities established outposts. It wasn't long before they had sailed all the way to Spain to tap the rich silver mines near the Iberian region of Tartessus on the Atlantic coast just beyond the Pillars of Hercules. The Tyrians soon established their own colony at Gades (modern Cadiz) just south of Tartessus, over two thousand miles from their Phoenician homeland. As the Hebrew prophet Isaiah proclaimed:

> Tyre, that bestower of crowns, whose merchants were princes, whose traders were the most renowned on earth.[3]

In their voyages, the Tyrians came as merchants and entrepreneurs, not conquerors, and established close and usually peaceful commercial ties with native peoples, including the Greeks, who adapted the Punic alphabet to write their own language.

The city that Elissa founded[4] was in the perfect location. Ships sailing from Lebanon to Spain and back again had little choice but to pass close to their settlement through the narrowed passage between the bulge of Africa and the island of Sicily. It also lay on the busy north–south sea lanes linking Sardinia and the wealthy Etruscan cities of Italy to the eastern Mediterranean. The mountainous coastal lands near Carthage, unlike the Sahara Desert farther south, were well-watered by rivers that could support fields and orchards of barley, wheat, oats, olives, fruits, and grapes. The city itself was established on the spacious headland of a peninsula that provided natural protection from inland attacks, but also easy access to the sea and the lands beyond. Local tribes were amicable enough and eager for the imported goods from around the Mediterranean which the Carthaginians could offer. Native people and Carthaginians intermarried from the beginning to create a new and unique African culture combining the ways of the ancient lands to the south and the Mediterranean world to the north and east.

Archaeology cannot tell us for certain if Elissa and her band of settlers were real, but excavations have revealed that Carthage was thriving by the mid-eighth century B.C.E. Fine pottery from Greece and luxury goods from Etruscan Italy are found in the earliest layers of the city. A defensive wall of stone soon circled the settlement—for no city in the ancient world trusted wholly in the good will of its neighbors. Early cemeteries suggest a population of up to thirty thousand within a century of the city's founding. The graves contained bodies buried with great care along with perfume flasks, lamps, and statuettes. Carthage not only imported goods from abroad, but soon made fine quality products of her own. Metalworking and pottery were mainstays for export via its growing merchant fleet, along with multicolored carpets and even purple dye from its local factories.

Carthage developed and nurtured its own trading ties with the people of Africa and around the Mediterranean from its beginning. Well-traveled merchant roads from Numidia to the west as well as Libya and Egypt to the east led to Carthage, as did caravan and trading routes stretching across the Sahara from the lands and kingdoms far to the south along the Senegal, Niger, and upper Nile rivers. In the Mediterranean, Carthaginian traders sailed regularly back to Tyre, but even more so to the west and north. Spain, Italy, and particularly Sardinia and Sicily were frequent stops for Carthaginian merchants who soon established permanent trading posts on these islands. When trade from Tyre declined after its conquest by the Babylonian king Nebuchadnezzar in the sixth century B.C.E., Carthage quickly stepped in to fill the commercial vacuum.

But Carthaginian maritime commerce and exploration were not confined to the Mediterranean. The merchants of the city had a keen interest in developing direct trade by sea with the more distant regions of Europe and Africa. Just after 500 B.C.E., two expeditions were launched[5] whose stories still survive, though there were certainly many other voyages. The first was led by a single ship commanded by a Carthaginian named Himilco who sailed north beyond the Pillars of Hercules along the Spanish and Gaulish shores of the Atlantic until he reached the islands of the Oestrymnians, perhaps on the coast of Brittany or Cornwall, that were a rich source of tin. From there, Himilco may have sailed on to northern Britain and Ireland. The second expedition was much larger and consisted of a fleet of ships and colonist families led by a Carthaginian named Hanno. The records of this voyage were reportedly on display at the temple of Ba'al Hammon in Carthage during Hannibal's own lifetime. Hanno captained his flotilla of ships into the stormy Atlantic and down the coast of Morocco, establishing new Carthaginian settlements along the way, including one at Cerne Island in present-day Mauritania, where a lively trade developed with the native people on the nearby mainland for lion skins and elephant ivory. After the last of the colonists were settled, Hanno continued south of the Sahara to what is probably the mouth of the Senegal River and farther yet, perhaps even to the Niger River delta and beyond. Along the way they were attacked by what they described as very hairy creatures they called *gorillas*, whose skins they took back to Carthage, then watched an erupting volcano called they called the Chariot of the Gods. A brief story told by the skeptical Greek historian

Herodotus that certain Phoenician sailors about the seventh century B.C.E. circumnavigated all of Africa should not be dismissed and may be only one of many sea journeys that regularly connected Carthage with a vast trading network all the way to the southern tip of the continent. But however far Himilco, Hanno, and other Carthaginians sailed on their distant expeditions, their voyages show that the Carthaginians were hungry for new markets and trade goods, as well as possessing a powerful sense of curiosity and adventure.

Nonetheless, Carthage was always mindful of commercial opportunities closer to home, especially across the narrow sea in Italy. Trade with the Etruscan cities in particular had long been important to Carthage, but in 509 B.C.E. the Carthaginians signed a treaty with a small town in central Italy[6] on the banks of the Tiber River. This seemingly unimportant settlement on seven hills had just thrown off the yoke of their last oppressive king. No one else at the time gave a second thought to this struggling state, poor as it was and threatened on all sides by hostile neighbors, but the Carthaginians saw promise for its future and made a pact of friendship with the new republic of Rome.

❦

The Greek philosopher Aristotle praised Carthage[7] for having one of the best political systems in the Mediterranean. The city was not ruled by kings like Alexander's Macedonia nor by a democratic assembly like Athens, but jointly by three different branches of government—elected magistrates, an aristocratic senate, and an assembly of the people—a system that provided a balance of power and offered checks on any would-be tyrant.

The two chief magistrates of Carthage were called *suffetes* by the Romans and *shophetim* by the Carthaginians—the same term found in the Hebrew Bible for the judges of Israel such as Samson and Deborah. Like the consuls of Rome, the suffetes were men of wealth and status chosen annually to serve as the chief executive officers of the Carthaginian state. The second branch of government was the *adirim*, or senate, of Carthage, made up of the richest and most powerful men of the land. Most of the senators were wealthy landowners and many were deeply involved in the merchant life of the city, which they vigorously protected. Finally the assembly of free citizens represented the concerns of the common people. As with almost everywhere else in the ancient world, women had no official voice in any part of government.

One thing that set Carthage apart from other ancient cities was its dependence on mercenary soldiers to provide its defense and fight wars. Most cities would hire a few foreign soldiers from time to time to supplement their citizen militias, but Carthage relied heavily on buying protection. This had the advantage of avoiding the expense of a large standing army, but it had the disadvantage that sometimes the mercenaries grew violent when unhappy with their pay or treatment—a situation which would in time cause enormous trouble for the city and particularly Hannibal's father. These mercenary armies were led by prominent citizens of Carthage, but woe to the Carthaginian general who failed to win battles, for he would promptly be crucified.

The streets of Carthage, laid out on a neat grid, were bustling and full of activity from before dawn till long after dark. Fishermen hauled their catch ashore, vendors grilled meat for a quick meal along the busy lanes, and bakers sold hot bread topped with honey and herbs. Housing for the common people was in crowded but pleasant enough apartment buildings up to six stories tall. Most wealthy families had spacious homes north of the Byrsa Hill in the elite Megara neighborhood, a place Greek writers praised as full of lush gardens and fruit trees. All the houses had underground cisterns to collect and store rainwater for drinking and washing. Carrying the water upstairs was the job of slaves, who labored both in the city and on surrounding farms. Slaves were ubiquitous in the ancient Mediterranean world, whether at Carthage, Rome, or Athens, and were of no particular race. Most were prisoners from the losing side of the endless wars waged by other nations in lands far from Carthage, but some were captured in pirate raids or born into a life of slavery. It was always a life of abuse and degradation, especially for women, but with hard work over time most could buy their way out of enslavement. In times of need, young male slaves could serve in the Carthaginian army in exchange for their freedom.

Religion was a crucial part of Carthaginian life. The many gods brought from their Phoenician homeland were worshipped with great care and devotion, often influenced by native African religious traditions. Temples to Eshmoun, Reshef, Astarte, and many other gods were found throughout the city, including shrines to Melqart, who died and was resurrected each year. But the greatest of the gods of Carthage was Ba'al Hammon, often represented by his symbol of the crescent moon. He was accompanied by his female consort Tanit, who as divine patroness of the city was portrayed on art and monuments with outstretched arms raised to heaven.

The most striking and controversial feature of Carthaginian religion—at least to outside observers—was the *molk*, or sacrifice, of newborn children[8] in the blazing fires of the god Ba'al Hammon. The Jews wrote in horror in their scriptures of similar holocausts among the Canaanite cousins of the Carthaginians. Greek and especially Roman writers competed with each other in their grotesque descriptions of the rite to portray the Carthaginians as cruel barbarians. The truth of what the Carthaginians actually did during the *molk* and how often they may have performed such sacrifices is difficult to say, but it seems likely that at least in times of extraordinary danger they did sacrifice children to Ba'al Hammon as an act of religious devotion, even during the lifetime of Hannibal and later. But then again, the Romans themselves routinely practiced wholesale infanticide of unwanted babies, especially girls, and performed public human sacrifices of adults to their gods as late as the time of Julius Caesar[9]—a fact the Romans rarely mentioned in their histories.

SICILY

As Carthage grew in both wealth and power, its neighbors around the Mediterranean began to cast an envious eye on the city. The Carthaginian colonies in Sicily in particular seemed like ripe fruit ready to be plucked. They began to wonder if even Carthage itself could be conquered by a leader daring enough to invade Africa. Everyone knew that the Carthaginians were by nature merchants, not warriors, who relied on hired soldiers to defend them. Whoever could conquer Carthage, or at least its colonies, could become rich indeed.

The thriving Greek city of Syracuse in eastern Sicily under its tyrant Gelon was the first to pick a fight with Carthage in 483 B.C.E. when a rival Greek ruler Terillus from the town of Himera[1] in northern Sicily was driven from power by an opposing faction and appealed to Carthage for help. The Carthaginian clan known as the Magonids, who had long dominated politics in Carthage and held valuable trading connections with Himera, encouraged a reluctant Carthaginian Senate to hire mercenaries to help Terillus retake his city. This was just the excuse Syracuse needed to proclaim the Carthaginians—barbarians who pierced their ears, distained to eat pork, and even circumcised their sons!—were invading the Greek lands of Sicily and must be stopped. The Syracusans tried unsuccessfully to rally Greek allies, but Syracuse was still able to crush the Magonid general sent to Sicily along with his army. The terrified Carthaginian Senate sent envoys to Gelon and gave Syracuse everything it wanted in exchange for peace.

But easy victory and peace bought with gold only serves to make an enemy more bold. In 397 B.C.E. the new tyrant of Syracuse,[2] a young man of modest origins named Dionysius, roused the Greek cities of Sicily against Carthage with a new call to throw off the alleged yoke of Punic oppression and to share in the easy wealth to be gained. Ethnic warfare began as Greeks across Sicily massacred their Carthaginian neighbors. The Carthaginian town of Motya in westernmost Sicily was surrounded and put under siege by Syracuse. With no hope for the inhabitants to escape, the Carthaginians of the town fought to the last man to save their families, but the women and children who escaped slaughter were sold into a life of slavery. The Senate of Carthage reluctantly sent troops to relieve Motya, but too late to save the city. Nonetheless the Carthaginians and their mercenary armies were eventually able to drive the Syracusans out of western Sicily and restore the independence of the Punic cities on the island.

By 323 B.C.E., Alexander the Great had conquered the Persian Empire and ruled much of the known world from the

Danube to the Indus River, all before his thirty-third birthday. He had captured Tyre by great daring and released unharmed the Carthaginians merchants resident there. Such events did not go unnoticed in Carthage, distant as it was from Alexander's new capital at Babylon. The city elders sent an envoy to his court with gifts and pledges of friendship. Alexander received the envoy graciously, but let it be known he considered Carthage and the rest of northern Africa a future part of his empire—by war if necessary. Alexander's untimely death cut short these dreams, but his ambitions in the west were soon taken up by other would-be conquerors.

Syracuse had a new ruler by this time, a ruthless tyrant named Agathocles. He saw war with Carthage as a way to consolidate power and fill his treasury with easy riches. After initial and unsuccessful conflicts with Carthage in Sicily, Agathocles decided boldness in the style of Alexander would be a winning strategy and so launched an invasion of Africa itself. When his troops landed near Carthage, Agathocles burned his ships to let his men know they must conquer the city or die. The Carthaginians had never faced an attack on their home soil and so were terrified at first, reportedly burning two hundred children alive[3] to beseech the aid of Ba'al Hammon. Their Numidian neighbors to the west with their fabled cavalry smelled blood and joined in the war against Carthage. But after a civil war broke out back in Syracuse, Agathocles abandoned Africa and left his soldiers behind to be bought off with silver or conscripted into the Carthaginian army.

A few decades later the Carthaginians faced an even more formidable foe. The people of Tarentum were desperately fighting against the Romans who were completing their unrelenting expansion southward in Italy. Faced with certain defeat, they called on a king named Pyrrhus from across the Adriatic Sea. One of the greatest generals of the Hellenistic world, Pyrrhus too saw himself as Alexander's spiritual heir and gladly accepted the invitation. He also brought with him war elephants—the first ever seen on Italian soil. Carthage was mindful of its good relations with Rome and sent them a naval commander named Mago and over a hundred ships with an offer of help. The suspicious Romans declined, though they did sign another treaty of friendship with Carthage. With great effort the Romans ultimately beat back Pyrrhus unaided, though he did win most of the battles at a high cost to his own forces (thus the term "Pyrrhic victory"). Seeking easier victims, Pyrrhus answered the call of Syracuse to join them in attacking the Carthaginians in Sicily. He landed on the island soon afterwards proclaiming himself the latest Greek savior against the supposed barbarians of Carthage. After a series of stinging defeats and no help from Rome, the only Carthaginian town left in Sicily was besieged Lilybaeum in the far west. But at this opportune moment the Greeks of Italy begged Pyrrhus to return and defend them against the renewed aggression of Rome. He withdrew from Sicily and fought the Romans again, this time on the losing side, with the Carthaginians providing naval aid to the reluctant Romans at more than one crucial moment. Pyrrhus eventually escaped back to Greece and died there after being knocked unconscious by an old woman throwing a tile at him from a rooftop.

Carthage was once again at peace and worked diligently in the decades after Pyrrhus to rebuild its colonies and mercantile connections in Sicily. The Carthaginians maintained their policy of friendly relations with the Romans and honored their treaties with Rome by pursuing only commercial interests in Italy. But the Romans, who now dominated the Italian peninsula, rebuilt their armies and began to look for new enemies to feed their growing appetite for conquest and the riches it brought. They gazed with envy across the narrow straits separating Italy from Sicily, but lacked both a pretext and the navy needed for a massive assault on the island.

Their chance came in 265 B.C.E. when a small group of Italian mercenaries took over the town of Messana from Syracuse and appealed to the Carthaginians for help. Carthage answered their call in order to keep the Syracusans out of Messana, but the Romans saw their move as a threat to their own ambitions in Sicily. They sent the consul Appius Claudius Caudex to Messana with a few boats he had scraped together from Italian allies, but he was caught in a storm and his little fleet detained by the Carthaginian commander, who offered to return both the ships and men to the Romans unharmed if they would henceforth simply stay in Italy. The Roman consul rejected the deal and soon crossed again, this time taking the city of Messana by force. The Romans now had a toehold in Sicily and weren't going to give it up. The stage was set at last for war between Rome and Carthage.[4]

The Romans were able to scrape together enough boats to transport troops across the mile or so separating Italy from Sicily, but if they wanted to take on Carthage in a widescale conflict they had to have a proper navy. Luck would have it that at this moment the Romans captured a stranded Carthaginian warship. Always resourceful, the Romans copied the ship and built their own fleet in just two months. The admiral of the new Roman fleet at Messana was eager for a victory and foolishly sailed his untried navy to the nearby Aeolian Islands to seize them for Rome. The Carthaginians intercepted the Roman troops, who promptly jumped overboard and surrendered. Their admiral was eventually ransomed and returned home, blamed everyone but himself, and was reelected consul, though ever after he bore the unflattering nickname *Asina* ("female donkey").

But Rome was nothing if not determined. They built another fleet and invented an ingenious new type of boarding bridge called a *corvus*, or crow. When dropped, this device hooked onto an enemy ship with an enormous beak-like spike that allowed Roman troops to then board and slaughter the enemy crew as if on land. It was a revolutionary development in naval warfare that permitted the Romans to quickly gain dominance against the Carthaginians in the seas around Sicily. They even launched a brief invasion of Africa itself under the Roman general Regulus and captured several cities near Carthage before finally being defeated onshore. Storms meanwhile had destroyed most of the remaining Roman fleet at a cost of tens of thousands of Roman sailors and soldiers. Still, the Romans by this time had conquered most of Sicily save a few Carthaginian strongholds in the west of the island from which they could not be dislodged. In 249 B.C.E. the Roman consul Claudius Pulcher took the new Roman fleet to the Carthaginian naval headquarters at Drepana in Sicily and prepared to attack. When the sacred Roman chickens were brought on deck for the ritual augury, they refused to eat the grain before them, portending an unfavorable outcome for the admiral. Claudius was so angry he threw the chickens overboard and shouted: "Since they don't want to eat, let them drink instead!" The Romans lost the battle.

The Senate of Carthage tried to break the stalemate by sending to Sicily a young commander named Hamilcar Barca. Rather than merely supervising the defense of what little Carthage had left in Sicily, Hannibal's father—using unconventional techniques his son would later adapt—launched a daring raid on southern Italy, catching the astonished Romans off guard. After this Hamilcar returned to Sicily and began a series of rapid strikes against the Romans from a base high in the mountains. But in spite of his victories over the next few years, the Romans rebuilt their fleet and destroyed what remained of the Carthaginian navy in Sicily. This was enough for the Senate of Carthage. They sued for peace and agreed to leave all of Sicily to Rome forever.

Unfortunately for Carthage, the city had employed thousands of mercenary troops in Sicily who still expected to be paid. These soldiers made their way back to Africa and camped outside the walls of the city determined to remain and cause havoc until they received the wages they were owed. Short on money, the Carthaginians found themselves besieged by a veteran army ready to kill them all and sell their wives and children into slavery to recoup their wages. Carthage quickly organized its remaining soldiers along with local merchants, shopkeepers, and even slaves into an impromptu militia and began a war that was vicious even by ancient standards. The stakes were nothing less than survival, with neither side showing any mercy. When the besieging army captured some Carthaginian prisoners, they had them castrated before the walls of the city, then severed their hands and broke their legs, and buried them alive. At this desperate point, Hamilcar was again chosen as general of the Carthaginian forces and began a ruthless campaign to crush the rebel army, igniting ever more ferocious reprisals from the mercenaries. After months of slaughter and endless crucifixions, Hamilcar and the Carthaginians finally prevailed.

Having watched all the struggle and slaughter was the young boy Hannibal, who would never forget the extraordinary sacrifices the common people made for his city and now held Rome responsible for the terrible price they had ultimately forced his home to pay in blood.

H annibal was born in 247 B.C.E., about the same time his father Hamilcar took command of the Carthaginian army in Sicily. We know little of his boyhood years in Carthage before he departed for Spain, but we can imagine some of what his life must have been like from what we do know about his family, city, and the turbulent times in which he was raised.

Hannibal's Barca clan had deep roots in Carthage and a long tradition of intermarriage with native African noble families. The Barcas were wealthy landowners with substantial agricultural estates south of the city. Although Hannibal spent much of his time in Carthage, he would have been equally at home in the rugged countryside, roaming the river valleys with his friends and hunting with his father, on his rare trips home from Sicily, in the forested mountains. We know nothing of Hannibal's mother, not even her name, but she was almost certainly from another of the rich aristocratic Punic families which dominated the city's politics or from a wealthy nearby African dynasty. With his father often away in Sicily when Hannibal was a young boy, his mother took responsibility for his upbringing and education. Hannibal was the eldest son of the family in a world that valued male children above girls. He had three older sisters, so it must have been a day of rejoicing when Hamilcar received the news, probably in faraway Sicily, that at last he had a son. Two of Hannibal's sisters would make fine marriages with important men who would one day be admirals and generals for Carthage, while one girl married a prince from nearby Numidia—an important alliance for the family and a personal connection to the African cavalry who would serve Hannibal so well in his wars. Hannibal's mother soon bore Hamilcar two more boys, Hasdrubal and Mago, who would one day fight for their eldest brother in the war against Rome.

The education of any aristocratic boy in the ancient world included reading, writing, music, mathematics, and many other subjects. His parents undoubtably hired the best private teachers for their son, including a Greek tutor from fabled Sparta named Sosylos. Greek was the essential language for any educated person in the Mediterranean world after the conquests of Alexander, so Sosylos instructed young Hannibal in the language and literature of his homeland. He would have also told him stories of great heroes such as his own countryman Leonidas, who died at Thermopylae defending Greece against the Persian invasion. Every student of Greek read Homer's poetry, so Hannibal must have known well the stories of Achilles fighting Hector at Troy and tales of wily Odysseus finding his way home. His tutor would have also filled the mind of the eager young Hannibal with stories of the conquests of Alexander. Sosylos became a lasting and influential figure in Hannibal's life who would travel with him to Spain and one day accompany him on his invasion of Italy, writing a seven-book history of the campaign. The work is now lost, but was used by historians such as Polybius to provide a crucial Carthaginian point of view on the mind and deeds of Hannibal.

Carthage, like Alexandria in Egypt, was a city of libraries filled with endless rolls of papyrus texts lining the shelves. Hannibal would have wandered these halls with Sosylos, selecting Greek works by Plato, Aristotle, Sappho, and Herodotus to read. But Carthage also had a rich literature in its own Punic language, which Hannibal must have known. None of it survives save for fragments of a single work on agriculture in Greek and Latin translation by a Carthaginian named Mago, whose many volumes were reluctantly admired by the Romans. But Carthaginian libraries were filled with other Punic works including histories of their city and the wider world, mythology and religion, science and exploration, logic and metaphysics. We know that one Carthaginian scholar named Hasdrubal taught philosophy in the Punic language for years in his native city before adopting the Greek name Clitomachus and becoming the leader of Plato's famed academy in Athens.

The exciting world of Carthage made it an ideal place for a bright and curious boy like Hannibal to grow up. Ships sailed into its harbors every day from Europe, Africa, and Asia, bringing traders and visitors into the rich melting pot of the city. It was cosmopolitan in the truest sense—a world city open to all without provincialism and always ready for new ideas. Although Hannibal would soon leave for Spain not to return to his home for many years, Carthage with its busy streets, vibrant culture, and its vision of a broader world would always be with him.

SPAIN

At almost the same time that Hannibal was getting ready to leave Carthage for Spain, a child was born in Rome. His name, like his father before him, was Publius Cornelius Scipio. He had the good fortune of coming into this world among one of the most ancient and noble Roman families, leaders of the senate and wealthy landowners. The ancestors of young Scipio had proudly fought for the Roman Republic since its beginning almost three centuries earlier. In those days Rome was little more than a small Italian town struggling to survive in a hostile world dominated by wealthy Etruscan city states to its north and fierce mountain tribes to the east and south. It was a violent world in which the strong ruled and the weak were devoured.

Rome fought constant wars for survival, first against their fellow Latin tribes, then against an ever-expanding circle of enemies in central Italy. Roman men planted their crops in the spring, sacrificed to Jupiter and Mars, then took up their weapons to fight against whomever threatened them that year. Theirs was an army of free citizens led by two consuls elected yearly, for the Romans were loath to give long-term power to any man. In 390 B.C.E., just over a century after the Republic was founded, the Celtic Gauls of northern Italy invaded Latium and ransacked Rome, leaving the city only after the Romans paid an enormous ransom. When some Romans complained that the price weighed out on the scales was too high, the Gaulish king threw his sword on top and shouted: "Vae victis!" ("Woe to the conquered!") It was a lesson the Romans never forgot.

The Romans waged war with uncommon courage and unforgiving discipline. A Roman stood side by side with his fellow soldiers, men he had grown up with and whose sister he may have married. When the enemy charged his line with screams and curses, he stood his ground and did not yield as he stabbed the enemy with his sword and spear and forced the enemy back with his heavy shield. He formed part of an unbreakable wall and protected the man on each side of him at all costs, even as his heart raced and every natural instinct told him to run away and save himself. At the end of the battle, if he survived, he stood exhausted but proud above his slain foes. He stripped their bloody bodies of armor and valuables, killing any of their wounded who still managed to draw breath. The injured among his fellow Roman soldiers were tended to, his dead were buried with honor, and any of his own who might have fled the ranks were hunted down and tortured to death.

In this way, year after year, Roman power spread across Italy. What set the Romans apart from Carthage and most states in the ancient Mediterranean was their ability to absorb other nations into their state. Former enemies were forced to become allies and served the legions of Rome in new wars as auxiliaries. A select few of those who had once fought against Rome could eventually become citizens, so that their descendants might one day stand alongside the Scipios as members of the Roman Senate. Because of this, Rome was capable of unlimited growth and was able to draw on an enormous and ever-increasing pool of men to serve in its army. But while honor and patriotism were rooted deeply in its national soul, Rome also became a nation addicted to war and the riches it brought.

⊗

At the close of the First Punic War, the Romans had demanded that the Carthaginians abandon all claims to Sicily as the price of peace. In addition, Carthage had to pay Rome an outrageous war indemnity of over three thousand silver talents within ten years, a price in modern times worth millions of dollars. The Romans had promised that Carthage would be allowed to keep Sardinia and Corsica, but soon changed their minds and occupied both islands in addition to demanding hundreds of talents more from the weakened Carthaginians—a greedy move even the pro-Roman historian Polybius condemned as unjust.[1]

Having lost Sicily and devastated by war and the recent mercenary rebellion, Carthage was in no position to argue with Rome. The Carthaginian Senate capitulated to the annexation of Corsica and Sardinia and agreed to pay the additional indemnity. But there was much disagreement about where Carthage could raise so much money. The conservative faction in the Carthaginian Senate led by a man named Hanno—who would be Hannibal's nemesis at home for years to come—urged caution and a withdrawal from risky overseas adventures. He argued that increased taxes on poor

Carthaginian farmers could provide enough revenue to pay off the Romans without the risk of antagonizing them.

But Hannibal's father Hamilcar and his followers had a much bolder plan. They had watched in shame as the old guard of the senate abandoned Sicily and then Sardinia and Corsica to Rome with barely a whimper. With Carthaginian rule now restricted to Africa, Hamilcar and his party felt the answer to both paying the Roman reparations and renewing the power and spirit of the city lay in bold expansion into a new land—Spain. The Carthaginians and the Tyrians before them had extensive trading experience in Iberia and knew the countryside well. The riches of the gold and silver mines of the inland mountains were legendary, as were the fighting skills of the native Iberian and Celtic tribes. If Carthage could gain control of the mines, they could not only pay off the Romans but fill their treasury to overflowing. With this new treasure to rebuild a fleet and with Spanish soldiers serving in their armies, they could stand against Rome in any future conflict. The prestige of Carthage and its power to resist Roman expansion in the Mediterranean would be secured for years to come.

But Hanno and the conservative faction of the senate would not listen to such ambitious plans. Now, they urged, was the time for Carthage to remain quietly in Africa and not risk provoking Rome. Hamilcar nonetheless began to organize an expedition to Spain without the senate's approval. Such activities could hardly be kept secret, but the conservative faction could not stop Hamilcar from launching what was essentially a private war with troops and equipment he paid for himself. Some may even have encouraged the expedition to rid themselves of a troublesome man who would surely meet his death in a foolish attempt to conquer Spain.

And so in the summer of 237 B.C.E., nine-year-old Hannibal set off from Carthage with his father and a small army. Doubtless,

Hannibal's mother tearfully embraced her husband and son one last time before they departed. War was a dangerous business and she knew it was possible, even likely, that she would never see either of them again. Her fears were well-founded since it would be almost forty years before Hannibal would once more set foot in Carthage, by which time his mother was likely in her grave. In any case, we hear nothing more of her again.

Hamilcar's army sailed out of the wide bay that sheltered Carthage and steered west along the familiar African coast. The mountains of Numidia rose to the south as the ships made their way day after day along the Mediterranean shore. The fleet needed to stop from time to time at friendly ports on the eight hundred mile journey to buy supplies and refill their water jars. For young Hannibal, the voyage must have been such a novel experience that he could scarcely control his excitement. Although most of his life would be spent fighting and leading armies on land, his Punic heritage was the sea. A curious lad always, he would have learned everything possible along the way about ships and sailing from the skilled Carthaginian crew, the best sailors in the world.

At last the little fleet arrived at the far western end of the Mediterranean along the African shore where a solitary mountain marked the entrance to the vast Atlantic Ocean beyond. The Greeks told how Heracles during his twelve labors had set up two pillars to mark the edge of the world, one in Africa and one across the narrow strait in Europe. As Hannibal gazed north across the passage, he could see in the distance this towering rock now called Gibraltar. The Carthaginians left Africa behind and struck out for the Iberian coast, then turned west into the Atlantic until a day later they came to the ancient Phoenician city of Gadir, which the Greeks and Romans called Gades. Like Carthage itself, Gades had been founded by Tyre centuries before and long shared warm relations with its sister city, as well as a common language and religion. Hamilcar and the Barca family undoubtably had many friends and allies in the town. Gades, which became the first Spanish headquarters of Hamilcar, was the gateway to the famed Iberian trading city of Tartessus and the mineral riches of Spain with the silver mines deep in the mountains to the east. Gades was also home to the celebrated temple and pilgrimage sanctuary of the Punic god Melqart, whom the Greeks knew as Heracles and Romans as Hercules. Melqart was a divinity especially honored by Hannibal's family, so father and son must have visited his temple soon after their arrival to sacrifice to the god and ask for his blessing on the dangerous venture that lay before them.

⚮

H amilcar's strategy in Spain was simple and ingenious. The mountainous peninsula was divided among countless warring tribes who hated each other more than any outsiders. They had long welcomed Greek and Punic merchants who lived in small colonies along the coast and who provided them with luxury and manufactured goods from distant lands. Many Spanish soldiers had even served as mercenaries in the armies of Carthage for good pay and were accustomed to taking orders from Carthaginian officers. Hamilcar knew that an all-out war of conquest would be suicide with his small army, but a slow and steady campaign aimed at gaining allies and playing one tribe against another as his forces grew could work. Following the proven model of Hellenistic kings, he knew that a small force of elite foreigners backed by well-trained mercenaries and a growing body of allied soldiers from local tribes could rule over a vast indigenous population, especially if the man in charge was willing to pay his army generously and wasn't afraid to take chances.

The Roman historians we rely on had little interest in Hamilcar, so the sources of his war in Spain are sparse at best, but we know that he began his campaign by winning over his Punic countrymen in Gades. From this base on the Atlantic coast, he moved east into the mountains over the next few years, adding tribe by tribe to his territory through bribery, intimidation, or conquest. Brutality was sometimes necessary to make a point, as when Hamilcar publicly mutilated and crucified a rebellious Celtiberian king, but such displays were measured and rare. Hamilcar's effective style of leadership, which Hannibal learned by closely watching his father, was to win the loyalty of his soldiers by treating them firmly but fairly and leading from the front, never asking anything of them he wasn't willing to do himself. In this way Hamilcar was able to bring all of southern Spain under Carthaginian control in less than ten years.

The native Iberian and Celtic forces of Spain that Hamilcar gained for his army were a brave and proud people who would serve his son Hannibal well in years to come. Foremost among these were the many Iberian tribes whose ancestors had lived in Spain since time immemorial. They occupied most of the southern and eastern parts of the peninsula and were divided into numerous tribes each led by its own king. Far from being the barbarians described by many Roman authors, they possessed a sophisticated culture that drew from both native creativity and imported ideas and technology from around the Mediterranean. The languages they spoke were not part of the vast Indo-European family that included Latin, Greek, and Celtic, but were older tongues which had been used in Spain for thousands of years and more recently written in scripts derived from Greek and Phoenician alphabets. The Iberians were a deeply religious people who worshipped many gods and goddesses in secluded groves and at sacred springs, but it was in war that they were best known to the wider world. Iberian nobles were skilled horsemen in battle, while the common soldiers were rightly feared for their lethal ability with javelins.

The Celts who fought in Spain against and eventually for Hamilcar and Hannibal were relative newcomers to the peninsula who had arrived from their homeland near the Alps several centuries earlier and spread across the north, center, and west of the country. Called the Celtiberians by the Romans, they were tall, shamelessly boastful, and absolutely fearless in war. Like their cousins in Gaul and northern Italy, they worshipped many deities such as Lugus, the god of many skills, and Epona, goddess of horses. They lived in mountaintop villages and raised cattle, which they often raided from each other. They were famous for the golden torques they wore around their necks as well as their unmatched skill with swords in close combat. Both the Celts of Spain and the native Iberians were formidable warriors, but they had little experience fighting against a large, organized army of thousands of soldiers trained to operate as a single unit. The general who could integrate them into his own disciplined forces would have an army that could stand against even the Romans.

Recruits for his growing army were crucial to Hamilcar's plans, but to get them he needed money. As he moved east from Gades, Hamilcar seized gold and silver mines and revolutionized ore extraction with new technologies. Mines that had been worked by native tribes with limited expertise were now put under the control of Carthaginian overseers who used slave labor and new techniques of hydrology and metallurgy to greatly increase efficiency and production. Shafts plunged deep into the earth and diverted rivers were put to work crushing and washing raw ore to extract gold and silver from the rock that encased it. The precious metals were then taken to coastal towns under heavy guard to be transported to Carthage or minted locally into coins to pay Hamilcar's army. These silver shekels cast in a distinctive Hellenistic style bore the image of the god Hercules (Melqart) on the front and a Carthaginian warship on the back. They became the new standard of purity and value in the western Mediterranean and helped draw skilled mercenaries to Spain to fight for Hamilcar. The gold and silver bars that arrived in Carthage[2] also helped to mollify any opposition to Hamilcar's adventure in Spain and mute, for a time, the voices of Hanno and other opponents. Not least of all, the money pouring into Carthage from Spain allowed the war indemnity to Rome to be paid off years ahead of schedule.

Hamilcar had in effect become the ruler of an independent Carthaginian empire in southern Spain, much like the Hellenistic kings who succeeded Alexander at the other end of the Mediterranean. He still acknowledged the sovereignty of the Senate of Carthage over his territory, but his wealth allowed him to govern with little oversight from Africa. Soldiers from around the Mediterranean began arriving in Spain so that soon Hamilcar had tens of thousands of men serving in his army. The gold and silver mines also permitted him to import dozens of war elephants from Africa, the first ever seen in the Iberian peninsula. The native Iberian and Celtic tribes were slowly won over by coercion or warfare so that in a few years Hamilcar controlled all of southern Spain from the Atlantic coast to the Mediterranean. He then founded a city named Akra Leuke ("White City" in

Greek) near modern Alicante that became his new headquarters for further expansion inland and up the Mediterranean coast of Spain. In a few short years, Hamilcar Barca had transformed himself from the defeated Carthaginian commander of the First Punic War into a wealthy and powerful Hellenistic king.

4

NEW CARTHAGE

Hannibal was raised in the raucous atmosphere of his father's army camps from the time he was nine years old until he came of age. It was a hard world of men filled with danger, combat, and solidarity among brothers at arms. Battle-hardened veterans chosen by Hamilcar himself trained the boy without favor or mercy in the deadly arts of sword and spear. Cavalry officers drilled him endlessly in fighting from a horse until the animal moved like part of his own body. African elephant trainers taught him how to ride and care for elephants and the secrets for using the intelligent beasts most effectively in battle. By day, Hannibal moved with ease among the Numidians, Iberians, and Celts of the camp, learning their fighting techniques, languages, and customs, knowing that he would need to earn their respect if he were to lead these men in battle someday. Evenings were spent around the campfires listening to grizzled veterans tell stories of the battles against Rome in Sicily and how, though powerful and relentless in war, the Romans were often arrogant and overconfident—weaknesses an adversary could exploit. Hannibal would have also attended his father's meetings with his lieutenants and stood respectfully in back as they decided which tribes to attack next, which to approach with diplomacy, how to assure there was enough food and water for the men and animals, which soldiers to execute for dereliction of duty, and the myriad tasks involved in running an army. For almost ten years, young Hannibal received the best military training imaginable for a future commander.

But not all of Hannibal's youth was passed in training for war. His younger brothers Hasdrubal and Mago soon joined him from Carthage and were among his closest friends for life. All were brought up from childhood to despise the Romans as their greatest enemy. As Hamilcar would say: "My boys are like lion cubs reared for Rome's destruction."[1] Other companions of Hannibal's boyhood who would serve beside him for years to come were another boy named Hannibal, nicknamed the Gladiator, a young man named Hanno, and a foreign friend named Mago the Samnite whose Italian hill country ancestors had long fought against Rome and whose father was probably a mercenary officer in Hamilcar's army. And like Alexander tutored by Aristotle, Hannibal continued his studies in Greek and other academic subjects under the best teachers, including the Spartan Sosylus, who had come to Spain with his Carthaginian pupil. Hannibal became so fluent in Greek that he spoke the language with ease for the rest of his life and even composed a military history[2] in the language in his later years.

In time Hannibal undoubtably visited the tents of the prostitutes who followed the Carthaginian army on its campaigns across Spain, but little is ever said of any of the women in his life. Not that this was unusual in the ancient world. We know almost nothing about the wives or lovers of most generals and emperors in classical times. It was a world dominated by men in which women were expected to be loyal, chaste, and invisible. As the Athenian leader Pericles famously remarked:

> A woman's reputation is highest when men say little about her, whether it be good or evil.[3]

Even when Hannibal would later marry a native Spanish woman called Imilce[4] as part of a political alliance, we know little about her except her name.

❧

H annibal grew into a young man learning the art of war from his father and was fighting beside him in battle by the time he was eighteen. At the end of the ninth year of his Spanish war, Hamilcar took Hannibal and his younger brother Hasdrubal on campaign not far from his new headquarters at Akra Leuke to besiege a stubborn native town called Helice. It was a small city and not expected to put up much of a fight, but it could prove a useful lesson for the boys on how to force a reluctant town to surrender with minimum loss of life, at least among his own forces. While Hamilcar was encamped before Helice, he sent away most of his army to winter quarters, including his battle elephants, after an initial display of his forces to the fearful Iberians hiding behind their city walls. He was expecting the imminent arrival of a large, allied force to aid in any mopping up that needed to be done, but the native chief betrayed Hamilcar and succeeded in driving the reduced Carthaginian army away from the city into open country. Placed in an uncharacteristic position of weakness with a superior army bearing down on him, Hamilcar took a detachment of loyal men and drew the enemy away from the rest of his forces, including Hannibal and his brother. It was a father's decision to sacrifice his own life to protect his children that saved Hannibal and his brother that fateful day. Hamilcar drew the enemy after him while his sons and most of his troops escaped back to Akra Leuke. Their father died fighting hand to hand against his foes in the middle of a river, knowing that the Barca name would live on and the lion cubs he had raised would someday lead the war against Rome.

At only eighteen, Hannibal was too young to take over the command in Spain from his father. The Barca allies in Carthage instead pushed through the appointment of Hamilcar's son-in-law Hasdrubal, the husband of one of Hannibal's sisters. Known as Hasdrubal the Fair for his light complexion, he was a loyal lieutenant, chief naval officer, and close confidant of Hamilcar who had served him well in Spain and as a frequent envoy back to Carthage. Roman historians imply that there was an improper sexual relationship between Hamilcar and his son-in-law, but this was a common and tiresome slander of opponents by Roman authors aimed at each other as often as foreign enemies. What little we know about Hasdrubal shows him rather as a competent military leader who was practical and perhaps more open to cooperation and compromise with opposing political forces back in Carthage than was Hamilcar.

Hasdrubal treated Hannibal well and was loyal to the Barca family, not pushing the young man aside as a threat to his own power. Hannibal was given increasing responsibility and military commands against hostile Celtic tribes in the mountainous center of Spain. Hannibal quickly developed a reputation among the common soldiers as a leader who did not seek special privileges or shrink from danger. He was, as even the hostile Roman writer Livy admitted, a model soldier and commander:

> Hannibal was untiring[5] both physically and mentally. He could endure intense cold or heat with equal ease. He ate and drank only enough to sustain himself, not to indulge his appetites. He could be wide awake or sleep at any time of day, depending on when his duties allowed. He did not seek a soft bed in a quiet place in which to rest but was often seen wrapped in an army blanket asleep on the ground in the middle of the common soldiers on sentry duty. His clothing was in no way different from other young men his age, though his armament and horses were the very best. He was equally skilled as a fighting man both on the ground and mounted on a horse, always the first to attack and the last to leave the field.

Hannibal had learned well from his father that the surest way to inspire men on campaign was to share their suffering and risk his own life to protect them.

Hasdrubal led the Carthaginian forces in Spain for eight years and consolidated Punic control of the entire south of the peninsula. He founded a city he named New Carthage (modern Cartagena) at a superb harbor on the Mediterranean that became the center of Carthaginian power in Spain. It was closer to Carthage than Gades and near the rivers that tied together the mining centers of southern Spain. It was, as Polybius said,[6] the chief ornament of Carthaginian power and symbol of the Barca family's control of Iberia.

The new city also attracted the attention of Rome. The Romans had been preoccupied fighting against Illyrians across the Adriatic Sea and Celts in northern Italy since the end of the First Punic War. They had paid little attention to what the Carthaginians were doing in distant Iberia as long as the reparation payments in Spanish silver continued to flow into Rome's treasury. But now, with Carthaginian wealth and power expanding so rapidly in the west, they began to grow concerned. They tellingly sent an embassy not to the Senate of Carthage but directly to Hasdrubal in New Carthage to draft a treaty defining the boundaries between the Carthaginian and Roman spheres of influence in the western Mediterranean. It became known as the Ebro Treaty[7] for the river that flows across northern Spain just south of the Pyrenees Mountains. The terms were simple: Carthage would confine its activities to the southern and central regions of the vast peninsula and not send armed forces north of the Ebro River. It was an uncharacteristically generous concession by the Romans given that it effectively acknowledged almost all of Spain as Carthaginian territory, but the threats Rome faced in Italy and in Illyria were foremost on their minds at the time, not Carthage, which they still looked on as weak and beaten. If there was trouble with Carthage in the future, the Romans were confident they could easily handle it.

Four years after the Ebro Treaty, Hasdrubal was murdered at New Carthage by a disgruntled Iberian ally. His brother-in-law Hannibal was now twenty-five years old and a seasoned commander who had earned the respect of Carthaginian and Spanish soldiers alike with his "daring spirit along with a quick and fertile mind."[8] He was proclaimed general of the army first by the soldiers themselves in Spain and then by the government in Carthage—but not without resistance. Already his father's adversary Hanno was stirring up opposition to Hannibal back in Africa:

Do you think it will be long before Hamilcar's son looks on the extravagant power and royal authority which his father took on himself and delay our becoming slaves to the power that Hamilcar has bequeathed to his family, as if it were his to give?[9]

But, for the moment, the center of Carthaginian power did indeed lie with the Barca family in Spain, and now with Hannibal. The young general was at last ready to take on the mantle of full command—with his sights already set on Rome.

SAGUNTUM

Hannibal wasted no time once he had assumed command of the Carthaginian army in Spain. He could not allow any doubts to linger in the minds of his men whether he was every bit as bold and capable as his father before him. He set out at a rapid march from his headquarters at New Carthage north towards the mountainous lands of the Olcades tribe.[1] Livy believed that this choice of his first foe was deliberate on Hannibal's part because it placed him closer to the powerful Iberian city of Saguntum, but it may simply be that the Olcades provided a convenient target against which to prove his mettle. The capital city of the Olcades, which Polybius calls Althea and Livy names Cartala, was heavily fortified, but Hannibal knew that if he could take it not only would he impress his men, but he could cower the remaining Olcades towns into surrender without a fight.

With "a series of vigorous and formidable assaults,"[2] Hannibal overawed Althea and forced its surrender. Nearby towns quickly submitted as well, allowing Hannibal to exact a rich tribute from the entire land of the Olcades. This bounty he distributed to his Carthaginian and allied troops on their return to winter quarters in New Carthage. At only twenty-five years of age, he had proven himself to be as skilled a warrior as his father and even more open-handed in sharing spoils with the men who risked their lives to fight for him. It was an irresistible combination of generalship and generosity, which would bind his army to him in the future.

Hannibal spent the winter at New Carthage dealing with the countless administrative details of governance and preparing for a new campaign in the spring. As soon as snows had melted in the passes of the mountains stretching across central Iberia, Hannibal set off with his army and forty elephants to attack the distant Vaccaei tribe.[3] It was a march of over four hundred grueling miles over high mountains and swollen rivers, but Hannibal was determined to defeat the last of the powerful Celtic tribes of the peninsula. With the Vaccaei under his control, he would gain not only more wealth and warriors for his army, but could turn his thoughts to the Romans, knowing that Spain was secure.

On arrival, Hannibal immediately stormed the Vaccaei town of Hermandica (modern Salamanca) and took it on the first assault, but the more populous and resistant city of Arbacala took weeks of siege and fighting before it fell. Hannibal made alliances with the surviving Vaccaei leaders, then packed the gold and treasures of both cities on his mules for the long trek back to New Carthage. But when the Carthaginians reached the central mountains on their return south, they were met by the fierce warriors of the Carpetani tribe who were joined by disgruntled Vaccaei refugees and fugitive Olcades soldiers driven from their homes by Hannibal the previous year. Even if the enemy estimates of one hundred thousand by Polybius and Livy are exaggerated, Hannibal was still greatly outnumbered by a dangerous coalition of skilled Celtic and Iberian warriors. He knew that if he faced their full number in an open battle he and his men would be annihilated, so Hannibal met his first great challenge in battle with the unexpected tactics that would become a hallmark of his wars against Rome.

Hannibal waited until night fell and silently moved his entire army, including his elephants, across the swift and deep Tagus River in complete darkness. When the enemy troops awoke the next morning and saw that the Carthaginians had retreated across the river, they assumed Hannibal and his men had fled in panic in the night. The Celts and Iberian warriors smelled blood and could not be held back by their commanders as they plunged up to their necks into the water to destroy the cowardly Carthaginians. Hannibal held back his men on the far bank until the enemy soldiers had exhausted themselves crossing the river, then sent in his cavalry riding into the river high and secure above the currents to cut them down as they struggled to emerge from the deep water. Those who managed to make it across the river were met by elephants that trampled them into the mud as soon as they reached the far bank. Finally, Hannibal ordered his entire army back across the river to attack and destroy those who remained.

Hannibal had laid the perfect trap and enticed his enemies into it. The Tagus River ran red with the blood of thousands of Celtic and Iberian warriors with only minimal losses to the Carthaginians. With the seizure of the Vaccaei lands and his destruction of an enormous enemy army, Hannibal had secured his reputation in Spain and banished whatever doubts about his abilities might have remained in the minds of his own men, as well as among the leadership in Carthage. As Polybius says, no one in

Spain after this point would dare to stand against Hannibal and the Carthaginians—except for the city of Saguntum.

❧

Saguntum (modern Sagunto) had been founded three centuries earlier on the Mediterranean coast of Spain by Greek colonists and had grown into a prosperous international trading center now dominated by native Iberians, who had built a massive walled fortress on a high ridge near the sea. It was over a hundred miles north of Hannibal's headquarters at New Carthage, but still well south of the Ebro River that by treaty with Rome defined the northern border of Carthaginian Spain. Many of the citizens of Saguntum favored the Carthaginians as allies since they had long traded with the African city and prospered in their mutual business connections. But other Saguntines saw Rome as the rising power in the Mediterranean and preferred to secure good relations with the Italian city. This Roman faction had appealed to Rome a few years earlier to mediate an internal dispute with the city's pro-Carthaginian party. The result was, unsurprisingly, that the Romans ruled in favor of their Saguntine allies at the expense of their adversaries, many of whom had been unjustly put to death. But with the Carthaginians now the unquestioned power in Spain and furious with how Saguntum had treated their supporters in the city, the pro-Roman faction of Saguntum rightly feared that their days were numbered.

When Hannibal returned triumphant to New Carthage after his victory over the Vaccaei and their allies, he found an embassy of senior Roman senators waiting for him. These included the former consul Publius Valerius Flaccus and the ex-praetor Quintus Baebius

Tamphilus. Coming before him in his palace, they immediately took the offensive and accused Hannibal of interfering in the internal affairs of Saguntum as well as threatening a city which, they claimed, had long been an ally of Rome and was thus exempt from the terms of the Ebro Treaty. They warned the young general to remember that Carthage was a defeated power very much inferior to mighty Rome. Check your ambitions, they chided, and stay away from Saguntum lest Rome rain down devastation on Carthage.

But the Romans had picked the wrong man to threaten. All of his life Hannibal had been waiting to tell the Romans exactly what he thought of them and now he could do so from a position of power. He had grown up in a family that had never forgotten the bitterness of defeat at the hands of Rome in the previous war, nor how the Romans had shamelessly manipulated treaties to their advantage. With authority and passion, Hannibal excoriated the Romans for their hypocrisy and greed. He warned them that their own treaty clearly placed Saguntum within the Carthaginian sphere of influence in Spain so that Rome had no standing there. The Romans were in fact the ones who had broken the Ebro Treaty by interfering in Saguntine politics and supporting the murder of Carthaginian supporters in the city. Finally he warned the senators that it was an ancient principle of Carthage never to neglect victims of injustice who sought its help.

The shocked Roman ambassadors gathered their robes about them and stormed out of the palace. They had thought Roman power would intimidate the upstart general as it had so often before with Carthaginians, but they realized now that this was a different kind of man who did not fear them. With the Roman legions still deeply involved in Illyria, they knew they had no hope of sending a large military force to counter Hannibal in Spain in the immediate future and certainly not before he could attack Saguntum. The ambassadors sailed off to Carthage and repeated their threats to the Carthaginian Senate, hoping it would be more malleable. The opposition leader Hanno and his followers were typically cautious and advocated peace, but they were overruled by the newly energized supporters of the Barca family who sent the Romans back to Italy without the accustomed submission of their old adversary. The Romans knew then that war was inevitable.

From a legal point of view, the Ebro Treaty clearly placed Saguntum within the area of Carthaginian control in Spain and thus Rome had no grounds to object if Hannibal interfered with or even conquered the city. But it would be naive to think that the Romans were concerned about following the terms of a diplomatic agreement more than any other expansionist power in history. They knew they had made a serious mistake in giving Carthage free rein to conquer Spain while they sent their own legions to war across the Adriatic. They had believed the Carthaginians were a timid people reliant on mercenary soldiers. Now they faced in Hannibal a threat to their overseas plans unlike any before. Saguntum was their last potential base of operations in Spain from which, when they were finished fighting in Illyria, they could launch a war that could take the Iberian peninsula and its riches for themselves. Without Saguntum their position would be considerably weakened. Of course, Hannibal knew this as well and as soon as the Roman embassy had sailed away he began his preparations to take the strong and well-defended city.

The march of the Carthaginian army north from New Carthage to Saguntum[4] in the spring of 219 B.C.E. took no more than a few days, but the Saguntines would have known Hannibal was on his way long before they saw the clouds of dust in the distance. They had long feared this assault was coming and they were prepared.

Aside from using the natural defenses of the city, the people of Saguntum had stockpiled huge stores of food and weapons.

When Hannibal arrived he rode around the city with his lieutenants and planned his next move. Hannibal was a bold general, but never an impulsive one. He knew the walls were too strong for a successful direct assault, so he ringed the city with troops and outposts to prevent any escape from within or help from outside. Then he began the slow and methodical conquest of the city through a constant barrage by catapults along with missiles fired from siege towers to wear down its trapped citizens. He also began an intensive operation to undermine the city's walls to create an entry for his troops into the town.

But the Saguntines were also determined and resourceful. They knew that in choosing to resist Hannibal they had committed themselves to either victory or death. Their most effective weapon against the Carthaginians as the months wore on was the *phalarica*, a large iron javelin with a three-foot head wrapped in pitch and set ablaze. This terrible weapon when launched from the walls could pass straight through an enemy's shield and skewer his body. Even if it penetrated only the shield, it forced a man to drop his protection and fight exposed to other missiles.

Hannibal himself was wounded while fighting on the front lines when a spear struck him in the thigh and forced him to withdraw from the field. But after the camp physicians tended his wounds, he was back at the fore with his army. In the eight long months of the siege of Saguntum, he left the city only once to put down an uprising among some Iberian rebels in the south. During this interval he left his trusted friend Maharbal in charge of pressing the attack.

As autumn began, the outer walls of Saguntum at last fell and the survivors retreated to the inner citadel—but their fate was sealed. When Hannibal and his men finally stormed the heights of the city, they killed most of the defenders, exiled others, and sold the rest into a wretched life of slavery far from their former home. It was harsh and unforgiving, but no more so than any other war in the ancient world. The Saguntines had known from the beginning what would happen if they failed and had chosen to scorn Hannibal's reasonable terms of surrender each time they were offered.

But the question still remains why the Romans allowed the conquest of Saguntum to happen at all. Granted, most of their legions were engaged in conquering Illyria, but it would have been easy enough to send at least a token force of troops to help a city they claimed was a beloved ally. Even Hannibal would have hesitated to kill a contingent of Roman soldiers and bring down the wrath of Rome on his head before he was ready. There is in fact a persuasive case to be made that the Romans knew exactly what they were doing in letting Saguntum be destroyed by Hannibal. With the Iberian town crushed by the Carthaginians, the senate could declare war on Carthage and proclaim to the world that it was doing so to avenge an outrage. In other words, Rome allowed Saguntum to be destroyed as a pretext for its own greed and insatiable desire for territorial expansion.

But it is also possible there was some opposition at Rome to war with Carthage.[5] The Byzantine historian Zonaras, perhaps drawing on earlier sources less partisan than Livy or Polybius, reports that a faction led by Quintus Fabius Maximus was reluctant to leap into conflict with Carthage, at least immediately. Since Fabius would soon become known as the wisely hesitant general facing Hannibal in Italy, it is possible this is a bit of inventive foresight on the part of Zonaras, but we might wonder if there weren't indeed some in the Roman Senate who wanted to delay the coming conflict until Roman legions were better prepared and positioned.

But however large the opposition in Rome may have been, the war party in the senate won the day and dispatched another embassy directly to Carthage to warn the elders there that devastation was on the way unless they handed over Hannibal to Rome to face punishment. Even his nemesis Hanno must have balked at such an outrageous demand that was clearly meant to put Carthage in an impossible situation. To surrender Hannibal would mean surrendering Spain itself and all the wealth and power Carthage had gained since their last conflict with Rome. It would leave Carthage weak, vulnerable, and subject to further blackmail by the Romans as they established themselves in Iberia and encircled Carthage. The demands of Rome were meant to force Carthage into declaring war while giving the Romans the appearance of being reasonable. The chief Roman envoy[6] sent to the Carthaginian Senate stood before the elders with his toga in his hand and told them to decide which side it would fall, whether to peace or war. The senior magistrate of Carthage replied that it was up the Roman to decide which way it fell. Then with a typical Roman flair for drama, the envoy chose war, which the Carthaginians accepted with a shout of acclamation.

And so in the year 218 B.C.E., Rome and Carthage were again at war. The Romans believed it would be a conflict fought in Spain and in Africa that would end with a Roman victory that would make it once and for all the dominant power in the western Mediterranean. But what Rome had failed to anticipate was that Hannibal was about to change the rules of the game.

GAUL

At the end of the previous war with Rome, a generation before Saguntum fell, Carthage had lost control of Sicily, Sardinia, and Corsica, the three largest and most strategic islands in the western Mediterranean. They had also given up most of their war fleet and now had no effective way to defend themselves at sea against a Roman naval invasion of either Spain or Africa. Outsiders watching the looming conflict between Rome and Carthage would have bet heavily on the overwhelming advantages of the Romans.

True, the Carthaginians had a very capable young battlefield commander in Hannibal of the Barca clan, but any sensible person in the Mediterranean world knew that Carthage had no real chance of beating Rome. The best the Carthaginians could hope for was for Hannibal to put up a good fight in Spain and pray to the gods they could use that leverage to sue for peace and at least hold onto to their African homeland. That they would ultimately lose Spain and its riches seemed inevitable. That Hannibal and his army would likely be destroyed in Iberia was the price the city would have to pay. The Carthaginian opposition leader Hanno and his conservative followers perhaps even hoped the Romans would rid them of the Barca family forever. With Hannibal gone, Carthage could return to its traditional role as a mercantile power that was no threat to anyone, especially Rome.

But in spite of their military advantages, the Roman Senate was taking no chances and planned an overwhelming war of destruction against Hannibal and the Carthaginians. Early in 218 B.C.E., they began to raise not one, but two armies against Carthage. The first would set out directly to Spain via land and sea to conquer the peninsula using the recaptured Saguntum as its base. The second army would sail for Sicily and then on to Carthage to conquer the African city. The manpower for these armies was vast, with a total of six citizen legions of at least four thousand infantry each, along with forty thousand allied infantry and over six thousand cavalry for a total of almost seventy thousand troops. In addition the Romans were building a fleet of over two hundred new warships, most of which were bound for Africa. One of the Roman consuls for the year, Publius Cornelius Scipio, was entrusted with the conquest of Iberia and the defeat of Hannibal. The other consul, Tiberius Sempronius Longus, would have the privilege of crushing the Carthaginian forces in Africa itself. The Romans also sent an additional two legions to northern Italy under the praetor Lucius Manlius Vulso to deal with the troublesome Gauls of the Boii tribe who had risen in revolt, stirred up by Hannibal's agents there. But neither the Celts of the Po Valley nor indeed the Carthaginians themselves were an object of enduring concern to Rome. The senate and the consuls had made careful, methodical preparations typical of Roman warfare and were ready to destroy their enemies with proven fighting skill and overwhelming military force.

Meanwhile, Hannibal was well aware that the Romans were heading his way and was making his own preparations. After the fall of Saguntum, he shared the spoils of the city freely with his troops and then sent the local Iberians among them back to their homes for the winter, rightly confident that they would return in the spring. He also dispatched several thousand soldiers to Carthage, including a contingent of his famed slingers from the Balearic Islands, to reinforce the home city and remind the Carthaginians who it was who controlled the military resources of their empire.

Hannibal returned from Saguntum to New Carthage and threw himself into preparation for an unprecedented campaign against the Romans. He decided to leave his younger brother, Hasdrubal, as regent in Spain and instructed him carefully on what to do if the Romans landed in Iberia. As for his own forces, he began to gather together a professional and truly multinational army. Africans, Spaniards, Ligurians, Celts, Phoenicians, Greeks, and many others all flocked to Hannibal to fight the hated Romans. Hannibal was wise enough not to impose uniformity on his new army, but allowed each ethnic group to fight as separate units wearing their own native battle attire and wielding their favorite weapons. This created a good-natured rivalry among the nations under Hannibal's command to be the most outstanding warriors, just as their general intended.

As busy as he was, Hannibal nonetheless took the time to make a pilgrimage to the temple of Melqart—Hercules to the Romans— at Gades which he and his father had visited when they first arrived in Iberia years earlier. There he sacrificed to the patron god of his family and prayed for divine favor in the daring campaign he was about to undertake. It was doubly appropriate for Hannibal to do so since he was about to retrace Hercules's mythical route from Spain to Rome. The Greek hero had swept across the western Mediterranean with great success and defeated the greedy monster Cacus who had once lived at the site of Rome. Hannibal was undoubtedly sincere in his religious beliefs, but like Alexander before him, he was also a master at religious propaganda.

Hannibal returned quickly to New Carthage from Gades and in the late spring of 218 B.C.E., began his march north toward the Ebro River with a force of ninety thousand infantry, twelve thousand cavalry, and almost forty war elephants.[1] His plan was as simple as it was audacious. He would lead his army over the Pyrenees Mountains into Gaul, then somehow find a way through the high passes of the snow-covered Alps into Italy itself. It was a plan bold beyond measure not simply because of the difficulties of leading a vast army on such a difficult journey, but because Hannibal was committing the Carthaginian army to fight a war in the Roman homeland without any promise of support or reinforcement. No one had ever dreamed of such a thing before—and for good reason. The Romans were the mightiest and best-organized army the world had ever seen. They had most of Italy either under their direct control or intimidated into submission, and so were able to draw on vast reserves of Italian manpower that far outnumbered what Hannibal could raise. But more than anything, the Romans were absolutely relentless in their pursuit of victory against their enemies. Even in the past when it seemed they were beaten, they never gave up.

And Hannibal was marching into the heart of their empire.

T he Carthaginian army crossed the Ebro[2] sometime in the early summer. Like Julius Caesar crossing the Rubicon almost two centuries later, Hannibal knew there was no turning back once the river was behind him. He was now in violation of the treaty between Rome and Carthage, not that legal niceties mattered at this point, since the Romans had already declared war. But more than any diplomatic implications, Hannibal was clearly signaling to the Romans what his intentions were. They had many spies and informants in Spain, just as Hannibal had in Italy. The senate and commanding consuls would have heard quickly that the Carthaginians were on the move north of the Ebro instead of taking up a safer defensive position in Spain. Although the Romans would not have guessed at this point that Hannibal would dare to march his army over the Alps into Italy, he was clearly planning to meet the advancing Roman army of Scipio in Gaul. This was a different kind of aggressive war than the Romans were used to from the Carthaginians, who had always followed a cautious path. But to the Romans, Hannibal's advance was a more favorable turn of events than they could have hoped for. The Roman legions would now be able to fight the war not in hostile Spain, but among their allied Greek cities of Gaul such as Massalia, which could easily resupply and support them. Things were going very well for the consul Scipio indeed.

Hannibal meanwhile was waging the first battles of the war against Iberian and Celtic tribes north of the Ebro. The natives were not going to let the Carthaginians pass through their land unchallenged. Hannibal in turn could not afford to leave unsubdued enemies at his back while he marched to Italy. He moved quickly to conquer the Spanish towns and countryside south of the Pyrenees, but it took several weeks of fighting he could ill afford. He knew from his scouts that winter came early to the high Alps and deep snow would block some passes by the middle of autumn. Still, there was no choice except to finish the conquest of Iberia before moving across the Pyrenees. The battles were fierce and there were heavy losses on both sides, but soon the Carthaginians had taken every center of power between the Ebro and Gaul. Hannibal then left his friend Hanno behind to occupy the area with ten thousand infantry and a thousand cavalry as a defense against the Romans entering Spain from the north and to stand ready to reenforce him in Italy. He also sent home thousands of soldiers from the troublesome Carpetani tribe who were threatening to rebel against him on the march. In the Carthaginian commander's mind, it was better to have a smaller, more loyal army than a larger force embedded with discontents.

The journey through the chilly Pyrenees Mountains was challenging for Hannibal's army because of the hostility of the Celtic mountain tribes they encountered, but the passes themselves were low enough to be free of snow and were rich in summer forage for their animals. Each of the elephants in particular required over a hundred pounds of food each day and could not survive long far from a source of fresh water. The weather became more seasonable and grass even more abundant when the Carthaginians descended into Gaul itself.

The coastal area of Gaul was familiar to Carthaginian merchants who had traded along the northern Mediterranean shore for many centuries. The Greeks had long occupied the area, their colonies including the large city of Massalia at the mouth of the Rhône River, which had been established almost four hundred years earlier to facilitate trade with the native Celts. The Celtic tribes themselves occupied the inland area between the Pyrenees and the Alps and far beyond to the northern sea. Like their Celtic cousins in Spain, they were never a united nation, but instead a collection of many dozens of tribes each ruled by a *rix*, or king, who presided over his people and led his warriors in battle. The Romans maintained friendly relations with the Greek cities of Gaul, including their key ally Massalia, but their steady conquest the Celtic tribes of northern Italy had made that land ripe for rebellion. Hannibal was well aware of this tension and was already fanning the flames of anti-Roman discontent through his agents in Italy. If he could win over the Celts across the Alps to his side, he would add a huge force already present in Italy to his army.

Scipio meanwhile[3] was slowly leading his Roman legions up the coast of Liguria and into Gaul by land and sea. He had lost time helping to quell one of the ongoing Celtic revolts in northern Italy, so that it was early September before he reached the delta of the Rhône near Massalia. His latest intelligence placed Hannibal and his army hundreds of miles away still crossing the Pyrenees, thus giving Scipio plenty of time to prepare to crush the Carthaginians—or so he believed. It was a shock when scouts galloped into the Roman camp and told Scipio that Hannibal and his men were already on the western banks of the Rhône, just four days to the north. Reports said the Carthaginian army was preparing to cross to the eastern side of the river. This was a serious threat to the Romans, not just because Hannibal had moved his men with incredible speed but because if he was able to cross the river he could outflank the Romans and cut them off from any reinforcement from Italy. This was the first taste the Romans had of what sort of enemy they were facing. Scipio called his tribunes together and prepared his troops for battle, determined to regain the initiative and keep the Carthaginians from crossing the Rhône. Since transiting a huge army across such a major waterway would have taken a Roman general many days, if not weeks, of preparation, Scipio again assumed that he had plenty of time.

Hannibal, however, was moving at a furious pace. Within two days he had bought, borrowed, or requisitioned every merchant ship, fishing boat, and canoe he could find from the Celtic tribes on the western bank of the Rhône, who were accustomed to sailing down the river to trade with the Greeks at Massalia. But waiting for the Carthaginians across the river was a hostile army of the Celtic Volcae tribe who were determined not to let them land in their territory. Hannibal's plan for dealing with them was ingenious. On the third night, under cover of darkness, he sent a large force of mostly Spanish cavalry upriver with native guides under the command of another Hanno, son of Bomilcar. They reached a section of the river divided by an island and there quickly built a fleet of rafts with the timber at hand. Then they slipped across the Rhône unseen and advanced in a wide circle south again until they were hidden behind the army of the Volcae. There they waited for their signal.

On the fifth day, Hannibal was in the lead boat as his men launched into the river. The rowers competed with each other to be the first to reach the other side amid the cheers of their comrades on the western shore. The Volcae sent up a deafening Celtic war cry as they waited eagerly for the Carthaginians to reach the eastern bank. But just at that moment Hanno's cavalry, having been roused from their hiding place by Hannibal's smoke signals, struck the Volcae in complete surprise from behind and sent them into a panic. Hannibal then landed the first of his troops on the eastern bank and joined in the fight. In very little time, the Volcae were killed or driven away and the transport of the rest of the Carthaginian infantry and horses began in earnest. By nightfall, only the elephants remained on the far shore of the river.

The western world had first encountered war elephants when Alexander the Great launched his invasion of the Persian Empire over a century earlier. On the battlefield the Indian elephants of the Persian forces looked formidable and could indeed cause havoc among terrified enemy troops, but in practice their usefulness was more symbolic than tactical. Hard to control and easily panicked themselves, elephants were as likely to trample their own troops as the enemy. But Hannibal and the Barcas had embraced battle elephants as a family mascot. No one is certain if his elephants were Indian or a North African species no longer in existence, but they were a smaller breed than the huge and utterly uncontrollable animals that lived south of the Sahara.

Hannibal's elephants were at home in water, but the Rhône was a swift, cold, and very wide river that made it impractical for the animals to simply swim across. But Hannibal had been working on the problem of how to get them to the eastern shore for a long time. He had his men make giant pontoon rafts at the end of a long earthen pathway built far into river, then covered these with dirt and vegetation so they looked like the rest of the causeway. Onto these detachable rafts he led two female elephants, which the remaining males naturally followed. When all the animals were on board, he cut the cords holding the rafts to the causeway and set them loose across the river. Some of the elephants panicked and jumped into the river midstream, drowning the mahouts on their backs, but were then able to complete the crossing by walking on the riverbed while holding their trunks above the water to breathe. The remaining beasts froze in terror on the rafts and were quickly ferried across to the eastern shore. In the end, all the traumatized but very relieved elephants reached the far side of the Rhône and joined the rest of the Carthaginian army.

Meanwhile Hannibal had sent five hundred Numidian cavalry south to scout the movements of Scipio's army based in Massalia. They soon rode back into camp and reported that they had encountered Roman cavalry just few miles away and fought a short but fierce battle at a cost of almost half of their force, though they had sent the Romans galloping back to Scipio with heavy losses of their own. Hearing this, Hannibal ordered his army away from the coast towards the distant mountains, not wanting to get bogged down in a war in Gaul.

It was now that the astonished Romans finally realized that Hannibal meant to march his army across the Alps and invade Italy itself. The very real danger to Rome in this brilliant and audacious move prompted Scipio to immediately turn his army around and return to Italy to recruit more troops to face Hannibal there, as it was unlikely he could catch up to him in Gaul. But, in a far-thinking move that would have implications for the war ahead, Scipio sent his brother onward to Spain with a large part of the army to occupy the Carthaginian troops there and keep them from reinforcing Hannibal from Iberia.

The Carthaginians could see the snow-capped Alps before them looming taller every day. Hannibal, ever the master of troop morale, had called an assembly of his army before they left the Rhône and brought forward an Italian Celtic chieftain named Magilus who spoke to the Carthaginian soldiers and assured them his people were eagerly waiting to welcome them on the far side of the Alps. Hannibal addressed them as well and assured them that victory against Rome lay over the mountains. The crossing would be difficult, he warned them, but no army on earth since the days of Alexander was better prepared for what lay ahead. His men had the greatest faith in Hannibal and cheered themselves hoarse at the words of their commander. Then they turned and marched towards the towering Alps, ready to face the greatest challenge of their lives.

THE ALPS

With Scipio and his Roman troops moving back into Italy from Gaul along the coastal roads, the more southern and lower routes over the Alps were closed to Hannibal's army. The only option for the Carthaginians was to head north along the Rhône and then turn east towards one of the higher passes. Hannibal led his men on a march north for four days until they arrived at a place where the Isara (today the Isère) River flows into the Rhône just north of modern Valence, at a place both Polybius and Livy call the Island.[1]

For over two thousand years historians have debated the route Hannibal took over the Alps after this point. Polybius and Livy, our two primary sources on the march, diverge markedly after the Island, and Livy in particular becomes difficult to follow. As is often the case, Polybius is presumed to be our better source, especially as he traveled much of the route himself and interviewed elderly veterans who had marched with Hannibal. But even putting our faith in Polybius leaves many unanswered questions about the exact path Hannibal and his army took over the mountains.

Whatever route Hannibal took,[2] the marvel of his success in doing so was not simply that he crossed over the mountains. Merchants, immigrants, and even entire armed Celtic tribes had been doing so for centuries. It was such an extraordinary achievement because he led so many men, tens of thousands, along with his elephants, across the unfamiliar Alps through the snow and ice of early winter while overcoming large armies of fierce and well-armed mountain warriors who were determined to destroy them. Such a thing had never been done before.

Hannibal's first step in crossing the Alps was to insure he had local allies at his back. At the Island where the Rhône and Isère met, Hannibal was approached by the elder of two brothers from the nearby Celtic Allobroges tribe who was in a dispute with his younger sibling about who should be the next king. Kingship in the Celtic world did not pass automatically to the eldest son of the late ruler, so it was a matter of who could win the most supporters, either by persuasion or military force. Hannibal saw an opportunity and threw his support behind the older brother. Together they easily drove away the forces of the younger man and secured the tribal leadership for the elder. In gratitude, the new king supplied the Carthaginians with warm clothing for the mountains and plentiful supplies, including new weapons and surplus grain that was now being harvested in the rich fields of southern Gaul. Not least of all, the new king gave Hannibal a large contingent of soldiers to act as a rearguard for his army as they marched into the mountains.

But Hannibal had knowingly made a difficult decision in supporting the elder sibling since his younger brother still ruled the eastern and more mountainous part of the tribal territory through which the Carthaginians would soon have to march. After ten more days Hannibal and his army arrived at the base of the Alps at a place where the river burst out of the mountains through a narrow canyon with steep cliffs on both sides. As Hannibal realized immediately, it was the ideal place for the hill tribe to ambush a larger force, since the Carthaginian army would be compelled to march through the canyon in a single line stretched out for miles. The cavalry would also be useless in such a tight situation, as would the elephants. To make matters worse, Hannibal lost his rear guard from the Allobroges' king at this point, since they refused to enter these dangerous narrows.

Hannibal sent out scouts who were skilled at moving silently through mountain terrain who reported back that there were enemy troops positioned in the heights above the canyon ready to attack the Carthaginian army as it passed below, though most of these men went back to their villages at night. Elevation was always a huge advantage in ancient warfare as it allowed soldiers to launch weapons and even boulders down a mountainside against their enemy, killing men and throwing an army into chaos. But Hannibal was an innovative general who was well-skilled at fighting Celtic tribes in the hills of Spain. As evening fell, he ordered the bulk of his men to remain in the valley below near the conspicuously blazing campfires while he himself led the best of his warriors up a rugged trail deep into the canyon above the positions held by the enemy troops. Silently Hannibal and his men crept down into each enemy post during the night and slit the throats of the Allobroges' guards left on watch. When morning came, the Celts returning from their homes found the Carthaginians in possession of the heights above the canyon. Hannibal had out-ambushed the ambushers.

But the danger to his army as they passed through the canyon was still very real. The Allobroges were not about to give up without a fight the rich spoils the Carthaginians were carrying on their hundreds of pack animals. Deprived of the advantages of height, they returned to the time-honored Celtic battle technique of a frenzied, frontal mass assault. With blood-curdling screams and swinging swords, they poured out of their nearby fortress and fell on the thinly stretched Carthaginian line halfway through the canyon. Many of the Allobroges were cut down in their charge, but they threw the column into disorder with horses and pack animals rushing madly in all directions while the Carthaginian soldiers tried to form a line against an attack that seemed to be coming from everywhere at once. Hannibal was watching from above and rushed down the slopes with his men to kill many of the raiders, but he still lost a large number of his men and many of his food supplies before he was able to drive the enemy away.

Hannibal reorganized the scattered train of men and supplies and led them into the broader mountain valley beyond the canyon, then turned back and stormed the lightly guarded Allobroges fortress. There he found many of his own stolen pack animals along with the stores the raiders had collected for the coming winter. Although his losses had been heavy, the food his men loaded on the mules would be crucial in the march ahead.

After staying the night at the captured fortress, Hannibal pressed on with his army higher into the mountains. Just a few days later he was approached by another group of local Celts holding out wreaths as a sign of their supposed friendship. They told Hannibal they had heard about his terrible vengeance on their neighboring tribe and wanted to make peace with the Carthaginians marching through their lands. They even offered to give him cattle and hostages from among their own number to prove their good will. Hannibal hesitated, for he knew how duplicitous Celts could be, but he reasoned it would be safer to accept their offer than to refuse it. He even employed them as guides through the passes ahead. Nonetheless, he didn't trust them for a moment.

His apprehension was justified two days later when a mass of warriors from the same Celtic tribe fell on the rear of his line as they were moving through a particularly narrow gorge. Anticipating betrayal, Hannibal had already moved some of his pack animals from their traditional place in the rear of the line to the front and placed heavily armed infantry at the back of the long column. According to Polybius, his foresight saved the whole Carthaginian army from utter destruction. But their losses were still severe as the enemy held the high ground and from it hurled stones and rolled boulders down the slopes onto the men below. Hannibal ordered his remaining pack animals ahead while he fought alongside his infantry throughout the night in an exposed defile of bare rock.

The next morning the enemy at last withdrew and Hannibal led his foot soldiers up through the valley to rejoin what remained of his supply train. His loss of supplies had been heavy, though he had managed to save most of his men. Still, his soldiers were growing desperately hungry. The stories of Hannibal ordering cannibalism[3] of his fallen men are almost certainly Roman propaganda, but there is no doubt that many were hungry.

For the next few days as they moved ever higher into the frozen Alps, the long line of exhausted Carthaginians avoided large-scale enemy attacks but were constantly assailed by small groups of hit-and-run raiders attempting to seize their pack animals and dwindling food stores. But again Hannibal was smart enough to put the most valuable supplies near the elephants knowing the mountain natives were terrified of these gigantic animals.

As they struggled onward to the summit of the Alps, most of the pack animals were slaughtered for food and supplies transferred to the backs of the weary men. Those soldiers too weak to keep moving forward were left where they fell, graves being impossible to dig in the frozen soil and wood too precious to waste on funeral pyres. To keep going forward seemed impossible, but to turn back in their weakened condition through the lands of hostile mountain tribes was certain death. There was nothing for Hannibal and his men to do except move upward through the snow and ice as the bitterly cold winds swept down from the high passes above. Men froze to death as they lay wrapped in the blankets of fallen comrades. Some who survived the nights simply refused to rise in the morning and were quickly dispatched by local marauders or torn apart by the wolves that haunted the alpine passes. And yet, day after day, Hannibal's army struggled ever higher into the mountains.

Polybius says that when the army at last reached the summit[4] of the Alps, the seven stars of the Pleiades cluster were setting in the west, as they do in late October and early November, and snow was piled deep at the top of the pass. For Hannibal it was a moment of triumph, but his surviving men were exhausted by cold and the hardship of the climb. The Carthaginian general gathered his soldiers together at the summit and showed them Italy far below. He pointed out lush the Po River valley in distance and told them of the Gaulish tribes there who were waiting to welcome them with friendship and abundant supplies of food and drink. He assured his men they were now scaling the very walls of Rome itself.

The army spent only a short time at the top of the mountains, then began their descent into Italy. But as dangerous as the climb up the Alps had been, the journey down was even worse. The pass descending the eastern slopes was steeper than the climb from Gaul had been and was covered with ice. Fallen rocks and boulders often blocked the trail, while a single misstep could send men and animals alike tumbling over the cliffs to their deaths on the rocks below. The soldiers spent much of their time and what little remained of their energy clearing a path for themselves and the animals. Wood for fires was difficult to find and food supplies were running desperately low. Pack animals and the remaining elephants were starving along with the men. And now, at the worst of times, the sky opened up and fresh snow began to fall, mixing with old snow and frozen mud into a layer of ice that made it even more treacherous for the army. Through it all, Hannibal moved up and down the line helping the soldiers clear the path and encouraging his men.

There is a story recorded by Livy[5] that says on the descent, Hannibal and his weary men camped on a ridge after clearing out just enough of the deep snow to pitch their tents. But their path ahead was blocked by a huge boulder that had fallen across the trail and made it impassable, especially for the elephants. The rock was too big for the engineers to move in spite of their best efforts, so one of the men came up with the ingenious idea of building a fire at its base. The soldiers somehow gathered enough wood and piled up the branches around the boulder, then set them alight. The alpine winds soon whipped the fire into a roaring blaze that made the stone glow red with heat. At this critical moment the engineers poured skins of sour wine over the glowing rock causing it to crack into smaller pieces. They were then able to push the remaining fragments over the side of the mountain and lead their animals down the trail.

It took several more grueling days, but at last the Carthaginians descended into the plains beyond the mountains where Hannibal finally rested his army. Horses and elephants grazed on the pasturage of the green fields while the men collapsed on the ground to sleep in the forgotten warmth of the sun. Hannibal sent out hunting parties to find food for the hungry soldiers. Polybius says Hannibal made every provision[6] to restore the bodies and spirits of his men. He also surveyed his army and counted his losses.

It had been five months since Hannibal and his men had left New Carthage in distant Spain. He had started his crossing of the Alps with almost fifty thousand soldiers. Only twenty thousand infantry and six thousand cavalry remained when they reached Italy. The loss of half his army[7] may strike us as an insurmountable loss that would doom Hannibal's hopes of defeating Rome, but the wonder is that he was able to get so many of his men through the mountains alive. No one, least of all the Romans, had thought such a task possible. No general would succeed in a similar massive armed march again until the time of Napoleon. Hannibal's army had been reduced greatly in numbers, but they were still a formidable army made up of some of the most experienced and battle-hardened veterans in the world led by one of the greatest generals in history—and now they were at the doorstep of Rome.

8

THE TICINUS RIVER

The importance of Hannibal's invasion of Italy went far beyond the devastating psychological impact it inflicted on Rome. It was a strategic masterpiece because it completely redefined the war between Carthage and Rome. Publius Scipio had already been forced to abort his invasion of Iberia and returned with most of his army to Italy to face Hannibal's army. And now the Roman consul Tiberius Sempronius Longus was quickly recalled from Sicily, where he had been preparing to take the war to the gates of Carthage. A conflict that the Romans had smugly assumed would be fought and won in distant Spain and Africa was suddenly uncomfortably close to home.

But even more dangerous to Rome than Hannibal's arrival on the near side of the Alps was the fact that Italy was not solidly Roman. The towns immediately around the city itself were loyal enough, but the vast majority of the peninsula was inhabited by nations and people who had no love for Rome. The many Celtic tribes of the Po River valley in the north were often openly hostile and some still at war with the legions. The central and southern regions of Italy with their Sabine, Messapic, Greek, and other native populations were often resentful of their Roman colonial overlords who seized the best lands for themselves, heavily taxed the poor farmers, and demanded thousands of auxiliary troops each year to fight and die in Rome's distant wars. Over a century after Hannibal, many of the subject nations of Italy would in fact rise in a bloody revolution against Rome that would almost destroy the Republic.

It was Hannibal's plan and mission to win over the inhabitants of Italy, vastly increase his depleted numbers, and deprive the Romans of a significant part of their fighting forces. His method was to employ both a carrot and a stick—or more precisely, a sword. Potential allies would be invited to join his army and share in the rich plundering of Rome. They would also be promised political independence, since the Carthaginians had long been known to have no territorial ambitions in peninsular Italy. But Hannibal knew he could not afford to leave hostile tribes or cities to fight against him. As in Spain, such natives would be both a deadly military threat and a dangerous example to others. Hannibal's punitive actions in Italy may seem harsh at times to modern readers, but they were effective and completely in line with the rough and tumble world in which he lived. In many ways, Hannibal was more merciful than most ancient commanders and a great deal kinder than the Romans had ever been to their victims.

Hannibal descended from the Alps into the wide plain of the Po River in the territory of the Celtic Taurini tribe, who would give their name to modern Turin. They were farmers, but also skilled soldiers as were all their Celtic kin. The Taurini had recently begun a war against the nearby Insubres, another Celtic tribe. Hannibal sent envoys to the Taurini chieftains at their town of Taurasia asking them to join him in an alliance against the Romans. Although they had no love for Rome, the Taurini flatly refused, reckoning that the Carthaginians were weakened from their march over the Alps and no match for the legions. Hannibal knew that if he let this refusal pass unanswered, his standing among the other Celts of Italy would be gravely weakened, so he determined to make an example of the Taurini. He gathered his army, surrounded Taurasia, and stormed the town. Soon it was reduced to burning ruins and the inhabitants massacred or enslaved. This harsh act of psychological warfare had its intended effect: almost immediately the neighboring tribes sent ambassadors to the Carthaginians pledging their loyalty to the cause and promising troops for the upcoming war against Rome.

But the Romans under Scipio had not been idle. The general now brought his army across the Po and cut the Carthaginians off from potential Celtic allies on the southern bank. Hannibal knew he had to act fast to force Scipio into a battle before the Romans could consolidate their position. But before moving against Scipio, Hannibal had an important object lesson he wanted to teach both his own soldiers and his new Celtic allies.

Hannibal called an assembly of his army and brought forward a group of heavily shackled Celtic men who had been captured while raiding the Carthaginians as they struggled through the Alps. These warriors had been deliberately beaten and starved over the previous few weeks so that they presented a pathetic sight to Hannibal's soldiers. He then placed in the middle of the gathering fine Gaulish armor such as their kings wore in battle, along with horses and decorated military cloaks.

The ritual combat of one man against another was an ancient tradition honored throughout the Celtic world, as Hannibal was well aware. He asked the young men who among them would be willing to take up arms and fight to the death against another of their number. The victor of the battle would be set free and given all the treasures he saw before him, while the loser, along with those prisoners not chosen, would at least have the comfort of death and an end to their suffering. Every one of the captives shouted that they were eager to fight, so Hannibal had them draw lots. Each Celt then prayed to his gods that he would be chosen. When the two winners were announced, both lifted their voices to the heavens in thanks, but those not selected wept that the honor had not fallen on them. The two young men then armed and fought each other with joy and abandon until at last one of them fell. The other Celts, as well as the Carthaginians congratulated him and sent him on his way with his prizes, but they equally praised the man who had fallen and envied him such a fine and honorable death. Then the Celts not chosen for the contest were led away to be executed.

Hannibal rose before his assembled men and told them he had brought the prisoners before them to fight so that they might see the simple choice that lay before them all in Italy. Conquer or die, he told them,[1] for victory or death were their only options. Retreat over the Alps back to Spain was impossible, while surrender to Rome would mean slavery or death. Those who died in the war ahead would leave this life in the noblest way a man might perish, fighting with his comrades in the heat of battle. Those who lived would gain not mere cloaks and armor but the riches of Rome and the glory of having conquered the mightiest army in the world.

Hannibal then ordered his men to be ready to face the Romans at daybreak and dismissed them. His soldiers all shouted in approval and went forth renewed for the fight ahead.

Publius Scipio had made a circuitous journey to meet Hannibal in battle. After leaving his brother and a large contingent of his army at the Rhône to continue on to Spain, Scipio marched quickly back along the coast with his remaining soldiers to Etruria, north of Rome. There he met the praetor Lucius Manlius Vulso, who had two legions under his command. Previously Vulso's legions had been sent to deal with the hostile Celts of the Boii tribe. Scipio requisitioned these men for his own army. In addition, he acquired skilled auxiliary javelin troops and cavalry from an allied Celtic tribe to provide rapid support to his heavy infantry. Notably, Scipio also brought along his teenage son of the same name so that the lad could learn the arts of war firsthand. This would be the first time the younger Scipio—who would play such an important role in the war to come—would see Hannibal and his army in action.

Roman engineers had already built a bridge over a Po tributary, the Ticinus River,[2] when Scipio arrived with his army. The flat grasslands on the farther bank of this small river were ideal for Scipio's cavalry, so it was here the Roman general decided to face the Carthaginians. He was confident that his relatively small but well-equipped army of heavy infantry in concert with his javelineers and allied cavalry could overcome the weary and outnumbered forces of Hannibal. Didn't Rome always beat Carthage? It was now simply a matter of teaching this young African general a lesson about the foolishness of invading the homeland of the Romans.

For Hannibal, the stakes of this first battle against the Romans could not have been higher. His army was alone and outnumbered in enemy territory without hope of support or reinforcement from Carthage. He had gained a few Celtic allies, but they were a fickle lot who would quickly turn against the Carthaginians if they didn't score a win against the Romans. His own African and Spanish troops desperately needed a victory as well to show that the suffering and sacrifice of crossing the Alps was worth it. In this first meeting—as indeed in every contest to come—Hannibal was always one battle away from annihilation.

The Carthaginians advanced east until they finally met the Romans on the western side of the Ticinus River. Both sides made camp not far from each other, while scouts reported back to their commanders concerning the enemies' strength and position. Tensions were high in the camps and no one slept well that night. Hannibal moved around the campfires encouraging his men, issuing last-minute orders, and promising that morning would bring their first victory against Rome. Or so he hoped.

At dawn both armies drew up their forces on the dusty plain facing each other. Scipio placed his javelins and Celtic cavalry in the center of his line, with the Roman infantry on both sides of them. His plan was straightforward and sound. He would charge the center of the Carthaginian line with his superior force and overwhelm Hannibal's men, opening a hole in the ranks through which the infantry would pour and finish off the enemy. He may have already been planning his triumphal march through the streets of Rome leading Hannibal in chains behind him.

Scipio's tactics would surely have worked if Hannibal hadn't read the field and seen in an instant what he needed to do. He placed his Spanish and his own Celtic cavalry directly in the center of his line to meet the Scipio's armored horsemen, who would be bearing down hard on his men. He knew he would lose some of them in the fearsome wave attacking his ranks, but he needed them to hold the line until his secret weapon came into play. Hannibal had placed his swift Numidian cavalry at both wings of his line with orders to race around the sides of the Romans and get behind the legions before Scipio's men broke through. This was easier said than done since the Celtic cavalry facing Hannibal's men in the center was formidable and the javelin throwers in front of them could quickly decimate a charging enemy with their deadly spears. Everything for Hannibal depended on speed. Interestingly, none of the sources mention Hannibal using his elephants in this first battle, perhaps because they were too unpredictable and might slow down an attack that had to advance with precision and swiftness.

Instead of waiting for the Romans to move first, Hannibal defied standard military tactics and sent his Spanish and Celtic cavalry first to charge the center of Scipio's line. The Romans quickly countered, but Hannibal had moved so fast that the Roman javelineers in the front of the Roman line were unable to launch their spears and were stampeded beneath the hooves of Hannibal's horsemen. When the two lines of heavy cavalry met in the center, there was a thunderous clash as both sides hacked and stabbed men and horses alike. The screams of dying men and animals echoed across the plain as the Romans met the charge and pushed back the Carthaginians. Hannibal's infantry on the sides clashed as well with the legions until blood turned the dry ground into dark-red mud. But the massive press of men made it difficult for Scipio's men and horses in the center of his line to maneuver—just as Hannibal had hoped.

Enveloping your enemy in battle was not a new tactic in warfare but it was notoriously difficult to achieve in practice, especially if you were outnumbered. What Hannibal did in his first encounter with the Romans at the Ticinus River was a foreshadowing of what he would frequently do in the coming war. The Carthaginian general took an enormous chance with a daring maneuver and made it work. While the lines were locked in the center, the Numidian cavalry had time to ride around both sides of the Roman lines and attack them in their undefended rear. The result was chaos in the legions. The Romans were suddenly fighting against the Carthaginians at both their front and rear. The Roman infantry panicked and fled, while their Celtic cavalry mowed down their own Roman allies to escape the slaughter. Scipio tried to rally his men from the center of the line, but was himself gravely wounded in the fray. It was only the intervention of the younger Scipio, who gathered a few men around his father to lead him from the field, that prevented a Roman consul from dying that day.

The Romans were now in full retreat over the Ticinus River bridge. The wounded Scipio gave orders to get as many men as possible across while Hannibal's Numidian cavalry bore down on them. He ordered several hundred of his men to stay behind and defend their comrades as they crossed the river, then destroy the bridge before Hannibal could take it. The survivors became Hannibal's first Roman prisoners.

Hannibal had not completely destroyed Scipio's forces, but he had soundly defeated the Romans in the first crucial engagement between the two armies. Word of Hannibal's victory spread like wildfire throughout Italy. Messengers quickly made their way to Rome itself with the shocking news and spread the dreaded word throughout the city from the market places to the floor of the senate—Hannibal had won.

❈

The wounded Scipio retreated back across the Po to the Roman colony of Placentia to recover and tend to his forces. The Roman government has recently founded Placentia as part of a long-standing policy to colonize conquered territory with loyal citizens granted lands taken from native inhabitants. Scipio's surviving men were stunned that they could have lost to the Carthaginians—men their fathers had soundly beaten in the previous war and who were supposed to be no match for the legions. All Scipio could do was to give his army a safe place to rest while he waited for reinforcements.

Hannibal meanwhile was having great success[3] in recruiting new allies from across northern Italy. Celtic tribes sent not only envoys to proclaim their loyalty to the Carthaginian general but supplies and contingents of experienced troops to strengthen his army. The Celts had decided that Hannibal's prospects now looked much brighter after his first victory over the Romans.

After a two-day journey, Hannibal led his army south across a bridge of on the swift and wide Po River after reportedly stationing elephants upstream from the bridge to break the current. He then marched his entire army to Placentia and drew them up beneath the city as an open invitation to Scipio for another battle. The Roman general was no fool and knew that Hannibal's cavalry completely outclassed his own, so he stayed safely behind the walls of the city. Hannibal assumed the Roman general would decline battle, but the foray was an important part of his psychological warfare against Rome and a key way to show his new Celtic allies he wasn't afraid of another fight. After this posturing was done, he took his army a few miles west of Placentia and pitched camp, welcoming more allies and searching for ways to build up much-needed supplies for the winter ahead.

Scipio believed he was safe inside the walls of Placentia with its many Roman citizens and allies, but he was in for a nasty surprise just a few nights later. His contingent of over two thousand Celtic auxiliaries inside the city—never happy at serving against their own people—waited until most of the Romans were asleep then snuck into their tents and killed a number of them before they could give warning to their comrades. They then employed a favorite Celtic method of showing triumph over their enemies by cutting off their heads as trophies, taking these bloody souvenirs with them as they fled out of the city gates. The Celts rode to the Carthaginian camp and presented the heads as proof of their true loyalty. Hannibal welcomed them warmly and added them to his list of allies. It was a dreadful blow to Scipio and to the morale of his frightened men, who now knew more than ever they were outnumbered in hostile territory. Not trusting the remaining Celts of Placentia, Scipio immediately withdrew his army several miles away near the Trebia River into a fortified army camp with deep trenches and palisades. There he waited for the arrival of his fellow consul Sempronius and his army from Sicily.

Hannibal's position was improving each day, but it was still the depths of winter and he had a large army to feed. He sent out agents to buy every scrap of food they could find from neighboring tribes, though it clearly wouldn't be enough. It was at this opportune moment that a man named Dasius, the commander of a nearby Roman grain depot at Clastidium, switched sides and handed his stores over to Hannibal. The Romans may not have been terribly surprised that their fickle Celtic allies would desert, but they never seriously considered that their own troops would betray them. Dasius and the soldiers at Clastidium,[4] however, were not Romans but were in fact Messapic allies from the heel of Italy. These conquered Italians had their own language and ancient culture that looked more towards Greece than Rome. They themselves had been defeated and colonized by the Romans only in recent decades and although they grudgingly accepted the rule of Rome, the stories of the freedom that their grandfathers told were still very much alive in their hearts.

For Hannibal, this was a gift greater than he could have hoped for. Not only were his worries of food for the winter eased but, even more importantly, he now had his first true Italian allies. Such forces would be essential for his plans to challenge the Romans outside of the Po Valley. But he also knew the war against Rome had barely begun. He had defeated one Roman army, but an even larger one commanded by the eager young consul Sempronius was now on its way.

9

TREBIA

Tiberius Sempronius Longus was a politician born into the Roman elite and a member of a noble family that saw high office and military glory as a birthright. He was also impulsive, impatient, and running out of time. The Roman system of government elected two consuls each year to serve as chief executive and military officers of the Republic, not trusting such power to any single man and not granting it for more than twelve months lest a man be tempted to turn into a tyrant. This meant that an ambitious consul had only a year to prove himself as a general and win victories in war. In times of crisis a man might be allowed serve longer in a proconsular position, but one could never be sure. Sempronius had only a few weeks to defeat Hannibal before his term in office expired and he was replaced by another man. This arrangement was both a strength and weakness of the Roman Republic as it discouraged would-be autocrats but also prompted ambitious and often inexperienced generals to take unwise chances in war to win quick victories.

Sempronius had been in Sicily preparing to invade Africa and so had to quickly move his entire army to northern Italy[1] when Hannibal invaded. When he at last arrived at the wounded Scipio's camp, he assumed effective command of the entire Roman army and sought to meet Hannibal in battle as soon as possible. Scipio urged caution, but Sempronius would have none of it. He wanted to beat Hannibal in glorious battle to establish his reputation and earn his triumphal parade through the Roman Forum.

Hannibal knew well how the Roman system of government worked and also how to take advantage of its weaknesses. He also had spies inside the consular army camp and in Rome itself to give him reports of what the generals and citizens were doing. If Sempronius wanted a quick fight, the Carthaginian was delighted to oblige him.

The Celts of northern Italy were never a united group and were always fluid in their loyalties. A few tribes were trying to play both sides by simultaneously helping the Carthaginians and Romans, so Hannibal sent out a small force to punish them by raiding their towns and taking their food supplies. The food was useful, but what the general really wanted was to push a few of the local Celts into running to Sempronius to complain, which they quickly did. The eager consul jumped at the chance to send some of his cavalry out of the gates to hit the Carthaginian raiding party before they could return to the safety of their camp. The Roman forces descended on Hannibal's men and killed many of them while taking back most of the stolen supplies. The Carthaginians sent out still more men, mostly Celtic allies, to attack the Roman cavalry, but was countered by Sempronius who launched the rest of his horsemen against them until the outnumbered and seemingly terrified Carthaginian allies ran away in full retreat, leaving the field to the Romans.

It was little more than a skirmish, but the small victory gave Sempronius the confidence that Hannibal's army were all inferior fighters and cowards. Hannibal had sacrificed a small number of Celtic allies, but put Sempronius exactly in the mindset he needed. The eager consul now harangued the recovering Scipio and told him it was the time for them to launch a full attack on Hannibal. Scipio warned him that the Carthaginian cavalry was still much superior to their own and that their Celtic allies were unreliable, but Sempronius would hear none of it. He was determined to meet Hannibal in battle as soon as possible.

※

I t was now nearing the end of December. Hannibal had spent almost a month encamped on the far side of the Trebia River gathering allies and supplies. During this time he had ridden out daily with a small guard and gotten to know the lay of the land where he hoped he would soon face the Romans. The Carthaginians had made their camp near the southern bank of the wide and meandering Po River which gave them protection from the north and a steady water supply. A few of miles east of the camp the smaller Trebia flowed into the Po from the south. It was a bitterly cold stream in winter with high banks on both sides. Several miles east of the Trebia was the Roman army camp of Sempronius and Scipio.

Hannibal liked the look of the land on the western side of the river near his camp. It was flat and would be perfect for a battle using his superior cavalry. The problem was how to lure the Romans to cross the Trebia so that they fought with the river at their back, thus hindering any escape. Any crossing before a battle would involve Roman soldiers wading across the freezing water up to their chests in full armor. Hannibal doubted that even Sempronius would readily commit his men to such a dangerous scenario, so he had to find a way to provoke him into doing so.

Battles in the ancient world were rarely fought in the dead of winter for the simple reasons that food was difficult to find and cold weather quickly wore down both the bodies and spirits of the men. Any sensible general would keep his men in the safety of camp and wait for spring. This is exactly what Scipio was advocating, urging Sempronius to wait until warm weather and spend the coming months training his new legions until they were ready to face the Carthaginians. Scipio also knew that Hannibal's Celtic allies would grow bored in the cold, dark days ahead and drift back to their villages if they had no one to fight. Hannibal knew all of this as well and would have taken Scipio's side if he had been a Roman, but he was a Carthaginian in a foreign land who needed victories. And so, Hannibal laid his trap.[2]

On his daily rides, the Carthaginian general had noticed a treeless area on the western bank of the Trebia not far south of his camp. It was covered with very tall reeds that could conceal numerous men and even horses. The Romans were wary of ambush from forests as this was a favorite technique of the many Celtic tribes they had fought, but a woodless area was not a great concern to them. It would therefore be a perfect spot for Hannibal to hide an armed force if only he could somehow draw the Romans across the river. Hannibal called his younger brother Mago, always eager for a fight, to his tent and told him to choose two hundred of the toughest soldiers he knew and have each of them choose ten comrades of similar spirit. When this force of two thousand men was assembled—one thousand each of cavalry and infantry—he sent them to hide in the tall reeds south of the camp during the freezing night ahead with no fires and in complete silence.

Before dawn broke the next morning, Hannibal made sure his men all had a hearty breakfast. It would be a cold day of fighting ahead if he could get the Romans to take the bait. He also ordered them to coat themselves with oil and fat as insulation against the harsh winter temperatures. Hannibal always took the greatest care for his men and they loved him for it. By sunrise his army was well fed, warm, and ready to face whatever lay ahead.

At daybreak Hannibal sent his Numidian cavalry across the freezing Trebia, having promised them great rewards if they could draw out the Romans. The water was icy but, since they were on horses, the riders were spared the shock of the cold water. They dashed quickly to the Roman camp and began shooting arrows and insults over the walls to taunt the guards. Sempronius was furious and ordered the whole army roused from sleep for battle even before they had time to eat. He had beaten the Carthaginians in the skirmishes of the days before and was now determined to crush them once and for all. Scipio urged him not to be foolish, but Sempronius would not listen.

The Roman cavalry numbering perhaps four thousand men chased the swift Numidians back across the river followed closely by sixteen thousand Roman and twenty thousand allied infantry— a huge army, cold and hungry but disciplined enough not to question a consul's orders. They plunged into the Trebia while the Numidians continued to yell insults at them from the far bank. The water was so cold that the soldiers were shivering violently by the time they emerged exhausted on the western bank in their heavy, sodden clothing. But there was no time to build fires and rest. Sempronius ordered them to follow the Numidians at a rapid march to Hannibal's camp.

As the Roman army drew near, they saw the Carthaginians drawn up in battle order waiting for them. Hannibal had positioned his Celtic and Spanish infantry in the center of his line with the cavalry and his remaining battle elephants stationed on the wings. Javelin throwers and his celebrated slingers from the Balearic Islands were stationed in front of the lines to hit the charging Romans with deadly projectiles before they could reach the infantry. Hannibal had at least ten thousand fewer soldiers than the Romans—but his men were rested, well-fed, and warm.

Sempronius and his army may have been weary, cold, and hungry, but they were still Roman soldiers. When they received the order to charge the Carthaginians, they hit Hannibal's men like a wall of iron. The tens of thousands of men who met that day on the winter plains of the Trebia knew that one side was going to perish. At first it looked like it might be the Carthaginians. The disciplined Roman veterans in the center of the line broke through the Carthaginian front and began to cut down the Celtic infantry in droves. But at that moment Hannibal gave the signal and summoned his bother Mago from his hiding place in the tall reeds south of the battlefield. Two thousand very tough Carthaginian troops suddenly struck the Romans from behind so that now the legions were fighting on both their front and rear, just as Hannibal had forced Scipio to do at the Ticinus River a month earlier.

In every battle there is a moment when both sides realize who is going to win and who is going to die. When Mago's men attacked the legions from behind, the Romans knew they would not escape alive. The slaughter was horrific as the Carthaginians surrounded the Roman forces and began to cut them down like wheat. Some Roman soldiers simply gave up and fell to the ground, though most fought on bravely to their last breath. A few Roman cavalry gathered around Sempronius and protected him while he raced back across the Trebia all the way to the town of Placentia. Where still-recovering Scipio was during the battle or if he even took part in the fight is uncertain, but he also survived the slaughter. We can be fairly sure, however, that his son, the younger Scipio, would have served as a junior officer on the front lines of the fight. From this vantage point, he learned yet again that Hannibal was a master strategist and tactician who demanded the respect of Rome if it hoped to win the war against him. It was a lesson that would serve him well in the long years of fighting ahead.

But the vast majority of the Roman troops and their allies did not live to fight another day. Those not cut down on the lines tried to flee, but were trampled by elephants or drowned in the freezing water of the Trebia as they retreated. For the Romans, it was a disaster beyond anything they could have imagined. For Hannibal, it was just the victory he needed.

THE ARNO MARSHES

Hannibal had destroyed a large Roman army in the decisive battle at the Trebia River and made himself master of northern Italy. Even though most of the troops he had lost in the battle were Celts, almost all the remaining Celtic tribes now eagerly swore their allegiance to him. Victory is always the best recruiter, and the Celts were hoping for vengeance against Rome along with their share of the plunder. The Roman civilians remaining in the Po River valley withdrew behind the walls of their towns and prayed to the gods for mercy. Hiding at Placentia, Sempronius tried to stop news of the terrible defeat and his incompetent leadership from reaching Rome. Eventually he dispatched a short letter to the senate informing them only that a winter storm had deprived him of victory. But the true scale of the loss could not be hidden long. When the news of the defeat spread through the streets of the capital, citizens panicked and were convinced, not without reason, that Hannibal would soon be at their walls.

Hannibal certainly had designs against Rome, but as daring as he was in battle, he was a careful planner who took the long view on the war ahead. He knew his position in Italy was still tenuous and he needed more allies. He also wanted to defeat single Roman armies battle by battle rather than launch a full-scale attack on the city of Rome itself. He knew from his experience at Saguntum in Spain that even small walled cities could take many weeks to breach through siege and starvation. Rome was much larger than Saguntum and had better defenses. It was more prudent for him to spend the coming months defeating the legions on the field and building alliances, especially among the occupied nations of southern Italy. The Celts were fine warriors, none braver in battle, but they were a fickle lot and easily bored in a protracted conflict. He needed steady Italians schooled in Roman discipline to fight alongside him in the time ahead. He also hoped that defeat in coming battles would increase panic among the Romans and cause them to make more foolish choices as he drew nearer to their city.

⁂

The two new consuls of Rome elected that year were Gnaeus Servilius Geminus and Gaius Flaminius Nepos, who busied themselves recruiting and training new legions from among Roman citizens and Italian allies alike. Rome itself was frantic day and night with the forging of metal into weapons and tearful supplications to the gods. The Romans were a deeply religious and highly superstitious people who took divine omens very seriously. In times of crisis throughout Roman history, many reported signs from the heavens warning of dark times ahead. Now, as told by Livy,[1] stories of omens and prodigies spread rapidly throughout the city and beyond. A luminous ship was seen sailing through the sky. The Temple of Hope as struck by lightning. Stones fell from the clouds like rain. The senate proclaimed nine days of supplication to the gods to win them over to the Roman side, including a generous offering to Hercules, the patron god of Hannibal himself.

Hannibal meanwhile spent the rest of the winter among the Celtic Boii near the modern city of Bologna. The Boii were faithful allies who hated the Romans with a passion and had long ago sent ambassadors to Spain to pledge their loyalty and service to the Carthaginian cause. They were also well-positioned for Hannibal's next step, which was to cross south over the central Apennine Mountains running down the spine of Italy and descend into the rich heartland of Etruria north of Rome. Although not as high or cold as the Alps, exactly where Hannibal might cross these mountains with his army was a major concern to the Romans and a question the Carthaginian general himself spent much time pondering.

There is a story about Hannibal[2] that winter that has long puzzled students of his life. Recorded by both Polybius and Livy, the tale says that Hannibal roamed his camp at night in a variety of disguises spying on his Celtic allies, hoping to learn whether or not they would remain loyal to him. Given that Hannibal had good precedents for distrusting Celts and probably spoke their language, it could be true, but it seems more likely it was a story spread among the Romans during or after the war as part of their general theme of Punic deception and trickery. Hannibal had an excellent intelligence network in his camp and had no need to risk his own standing among his allies by playing such games.

In fact, Hannibal worked very hard to build confidence among the Celts and other potential Italian allies. He made a point of treating his Roman prisoners harshly and feeding them just enough to keep them alive. In a deliberate contrast, he showed great kindness to the captives who came from pro-Roman Celtic tribes and Italian nations. In his winter quarters he called an assembly of all his prisoners and spoke to them of the cruelty and faithlessness of the Romans, reassuring them that he hadn't come to make war on them, only Rome. His motive, he claimed, was freedom for all people who had been abused for so long by the imperialism of the Roman state. Rome was like a cancer spreading across the Mediterranean, devouring nations and their ancient liberties in its hunger and greed. Carthage, on the other hand, had been trading with Italy for centuries and had never tried to conquer them. He did not claim that his motives were purely altruistic, for they wouldn't have believed that. He clearly wanted to defeat Rome to benefit Carthage, but the Italians had every reason to help him—because it also benefited them. When he had finished his speech, he ordered their chains to be broken and all non-Roman prisoners to be set free without ransom to return to their tribes and cities. Tell your countrymen, he said, what you have seen and how you have been treated here, then let all of you freely choose which side to follow in the war ahead.

When spring finally arrived in the Italian countryside, Hannibal broke camp among the Boii and began to move his army south over the Apennines. The northern Italian winter had been especially hard on Hannibal's elephants, so that in the end only one had survived.

Hannibal's exact route over the mountains is uncertain, but we know he chose not to lead his men along an easier route closer to the coast. The one thing the Romans were learning they could count on regarding Hannibal was that he would always do the unexpected. But for the Carthaginian troops who had crossed

the winter Alps, the lingering snows of late spring in the Apennines were hardly a concern. Once over the mountains, Hannibal
took another unforeseen turn and headed up the Arno River
valley. The Romans would never have anticipated this because the
Arno was still flooded with winter snowmelt and thus surrounded by deep and almost impenetrable marshes into which
no ordinary commander would lead his army. But Hannibal
was no ordinary commander. Crossing the marshes gave the
Carthaginians an enormous military advantage by avoiding
Roman encampments and would allow them to take the legions
completely by surprise. But only if they could actually do it.

His decision to cross the Arno marshes[3] was one of the most
dangerous choices of the entire war and a move that historians debate
to this day. When news spread through the Carthaginian camp
that they would be marching through these infamous quagmires
and bogs, the men were reluctant to begin no matter how much
they trusted their general. But Hannibal assured them he had made
careful investigations and found that the water they would have to
wade through was shallow with a solid bottom. And so the Carthaginian army moved forward, following Hannibal as he reportedly
rode high above them on the single surviving elephant, an Asian
beast with a broken tusk named Suros.

Hannibal placed his experienced African and Spanish troops
in the front of the marching line, knowing they would follow him
anywhere. The pack animals were spread out along the whole
army so that the troops had ready access to supplies. The more
questionable Celtic allies he positioned in the center of the march
with his deadly Numidian cavalry bringing up the rear under the
command of his brother Mago. If the Celts decided they wanted
to run away, they would have a difficult time sandwiched as they
were between his loyal forces. Sneaking away into the night, as

some Celtic allies must have tried, would mean getting lost and perishing in the trackless swamps. The Celts may have regretted joining Hannibal as they slogged their way through the mud, but they had no escape.

For four endless days and nights tens of thousands of men trudged through cold, stinking water up to their knees and sometimes to their necks. There was no dry ground on which to make camp at night and no fresh water. The pack animals spread throughout the Carthaginian line frequently became stuck in the mud and unable to move, with most of them perishing. Hannibal wasn't particularly concerned about losing the animals and supplies in the crossing as he reasoned they would have no trouble gathering enough food from the Italian countryside.

The crossing of the marshes was exhausting beyond description for Hannibal's soldiers. Their clothing became laden with water and mud, the excrement of an entire army floated around them, and warm fires became a fond memory. The effort of struggling through the endless swamp was much greater than a march on dry land. At night, their only option was to try to sleep standing or to collapse on top of the dead animals they arranged in piles so that they stood above the water. Supplies were quickly fouled and drinking swamp water made desperately thirsty men violently ill. Many soldiers became sick and feverish. Their companions tried to help them along at first, but they had little strength left for themselves and reluctantly abandoned them to sink into the mire.

Hannibal was not a leader to avoid sharing the suffering of his men, so it is unlikely he spent much time riding his elephant through the swamp. He was surely there on the ground encouraging his men every step of the way and enduring all that they did. Like many of his men, he was struck by a painful inflammation in one eye caused by the dirty swamp water. The only treatment was to irrigate the eye with clean water and apply a dry poultice, neither of which was practicable in the situation. Nor was it likely Hannibal would indulge himself with a special treatment unavailable to his men. As a result, Hannibal permanently lost the sight in one eye. Not above exploiting a misfortune, in the future Hannibal would play up his disfigurement likening himself to distinguished one-eyed generals of the past like Philip, father of Alexander the Great.

After four tortuous days in the marshes, the army of Hannibal finally emerged from the swamp somewhere near modern city of Florence. The men collapsed onto the dry ground, knowing they had once again done the impossible. Despite the incredible hardship his soldiers had suffered and the losses to his army, Hannibal had successfully led them through terrain no one thought could be crossed and had evaded even the most dedicated of Roman scouts. He ordered his army to take a well-deserved rest for a few days to regain their strength. It was a missed opportunity for the Romans, for if they had attacked Hannibal as he emerged from the marshes, the exhausted Carthaginians would have been destroyed and the war ended.

Many at the time and in the centuries since have questioned whether Hannibal's march through the Arno marshes was worth the horrendous suffering and losses, or if perhaps the master strategist had simply made a terrible miscalculation. The answer must lie in the benefits the crossing had given him. He was now deep in undefended Roman territory far from where the legions had expected him to be, giving him considerable leverage in positioning himself for the battles that lay ahead. His Celtic allies had suffered terribly in the swamps and many would have undoubtably deserted him during the march if they had been able, but to their delight they now found themselves in rich Roman lands filled with farms and villages to raid. They could at last turn the tables on Rome which had for so many years ravaged their lands and killed their people. It is doubtful that Hannibal did anything to discourage them as they pillaged the countryside. The Carthaginians had also lost most of their pack animals and supplies in the marshes, but now in Tuscany they could easily and quickly seize all the animals and grain they needed to replace them. Like so much of what Hannibal did in the wars he fought, his crossing of the Arno marshes was a huge gamble which could have resulted in disaster for the Carthaginians, but instead gave him an enormous strategic advantage that he could turn into victory.

LAKE TRASIMENE

The Romans had not been idle since their loss several months earlier at the Trebia River. The armies of Sempronius and Scipio had been taken over by the new consuls Servilius and Flaminius, who based themselves north of Rome. During the winter they had recruited thousands of new troops in Italy and even received a contingent of Cretan archers on loan from King Hiero of Syracuse. The two legions under Gnaeus Scipio sent by his brother at the Rhône the previous autumn had reached Spain while other Roman troops had been dispatched to Sicily and Sardinia to defend those islands against any possible Carthaginian designs. The senate also sent garrisons to occupy suspect cities of southern Italy, including the port of Tarentum, betraying to all their concerns about the loyalty of their Italian allies. The ease with which the Romans were able to replenish their armies with new recruits was a constant concern to Hannibal, who was limited to stealing allies from Rome to gain more soldiers.

The consul Flaminius set up his camp at Arretium in eastern Tuscany along the main route to Rome. He knew the area well since he had built a major road there, which he had modestly named the Via Flaminia, just three years earlier while he was serving as censor. His plan was to force Hannibal into battle and win the glory of defeating this upstart invader, preferably without any help from his fellow consul Servilius. Hannibal, a careful student of psychology, was eager to face such an arrogant commander. Polybius describes his method:

> Whoever is in command of an army must try to discover in an enemy's general not the exposed parts of his body but the weaknesses in his mind.

Not that Flaminius was without military talent, for he was an experienced soldier who had been the first general to lead a Roman army across the Po River several years earlier and had successfully crushed Celtic resistance in the area. But Hannibal also knew from his sources that Flaminius was that rarest of Roman consuls—a *novus homo*, or new man, who had no grand and noble ancestry stretching back to the foundation of the Republic. He was the first of his family to claw his way up the rank of Roman offices known as the *cursus honorum*. He had accomplished this considerable achievement not by blood right and patronage from noble families of the city but by skill and sheer determination. He had made himself a champion of the common people against the greed of the senate and the wealthy elite of Rome. At the start of his political career, the legions had conquered and confiscated the vast and lands of the Celtic Senones tribe, and the nobility of Rome had expected to seize the lion's share for themselves to build vast new estates. Instead Flaminius, as a low-ranking tribune of the plebs, had pushed a bill through the popular assembly to grant the new territory in small lots to needy Roman citizens. In doing so he had won the implacable hatred of the senators, who had done everything possible to destroy his career in spite of his abilities. He was also something of a religious rationalist who often neglected the tedious rites and auspices so important to the Roman elite. Now serving as consul for the second time, Flaminius desperately wanted to be the one to defeat the Carthaginians to prove his worth once and for all to the senate and people of Rome. Such a burning desire for victory was a weakness Hannibal knew he could exploit.

⚜

Hannibal had gathered an army of perhaps forty thousand soldiers during his first winter in Italy, at least half of whom were Celtic recruits that supplemented his core troops from Africa and Spain. In June he led them all out of his camp near Florence and began to move south across Tuscany toward Rome and the army of Flaminius. The Roman consul had a smaller force of about twenty-five thousand men at his command, some of whom were wary veterans of previous battles against the Carthaginians. Any prudent general would wait until his fellow consul could join him with additional men before engaging the Carthaginians, so Hannibal had to find a way to provoke Flaminius[1] into a fight quickly. He did this by marching his army contemptuously past the walls of Flaminius's camp and ransacking the rich Etruscan countryside around him. He burned every farm he could find and torched fields throughout the hills and valleys.

Flaminius was furious, all the more so since this was a land he had worked hard to improve with his grand road. His lieutenants pleaded with him not to take the bait in what was obviously a ploy to draw the Romans into battle before reinforcements arrived, but the scorched-earth policy of Hannibal struck deeply at Flaminius and his wounded pride. Moreover, Hannibal's army was now positioned between him and Rome, placing the city itself in danger and making him appear as a coward to his many detractors if he didn't take action. Flaminius ignored his advisors and ordered his army to follow hard on the Carthaginians. The veteran centurions, always the heart of a Roman army, must have shaken their heads in disbelief at such foolishness, but they were disciplined soldiers and so roused their men to action.

With Flaminius following closely behind, Hannibal suddenly turned east into a pass between steep hills to the north and the broad Lake Trasimene to the south. The narrow strip of land between the hills and the lake opened slightly as the Carthaginians marched along the northern shore, but there was little room for an army to spread out. The road along which the invading army marched continued around the eastern shore of the lake where Hannibal made his camp for the night in full view of the Roman scouts across the water. Flaminius was no fool, but since he could see the Carthaginian campfires in the distance he didn't hesitate to make his own camp at the mouth of the pass on the west side of the lake, blocking the Carthaginians from escaping in that direction. In the morning, he would follow Hannibal along the north shore of the lake and try to catch the Carthaginians unprepared. With a little luck, the narrow space between the hills and the lake could nullify Hannibal's numerical advantage in battle and bring victory to Flaminius.

But unknown to Flaminius, instead of spending the night resting in his camp on the far side, Hannibal ordered his troop to

double back along the north shore of the lake and position themselves in the hills just above the road. His plan was simple, but it
depended on Flaminius being eager enough to take the bait. He
commanded all his men, including the rowdy Celts, to stay hidden
with no fires in absolute silence above the road on which the legions
would have to march eastward in the morning. During the night
Hannibal kept hundreds of campfires burning on the far end of
the lake to assure the Romans that his Carthaginians were resting
peacefully in their tents.

Before dawn broke the next day, Flaminius ordered his
troops to pursue Hannibal. As often happens during the Tuscan
summer, a dense fog lay across the lake and covered the road
along the northern shore. It was impossible for the legions to see
more than a few feet ahead of them as they marched into what
even the least experienced soldier could see was a perilous situation. But Flaminius was confident that he could use the fog to
his own advantage to surprise the Carthaginians in their camp
and score a resounding victory against Hannibal that would
forever silence his critics in Rome. He had even brought along
cartloads of manacles and chains to march the Carthaginians
he graciously spared back to Rome as slaves. The thought that
forty thousand eager enemy troops were waiting in the hills just
above him never crossed his mind.

The road along the northern shore of the lake was so narrow
that the Romans were forced to spread out in a thin line that
stretched for at least two miles. At just the moment when the last
of the Roman line had moved beyond the pass and reached the
lake, Hannibal gave the signal to strike. Out of the hills poured
thousands of screaming Celts along with African and Spanish
soldiers. The surprised and outnumbered Romans were suddenly
fighting on three sides as they were trapped between the lake

and the hills. The fog carried sound in all directions and made it impossible to see where the enemy was coming from. There was no time or room to fall into battle formation as the Roman officers tried in vain to organize their soldiers into a defensive line. The fight quickly became every man for himself as they were cut down in the cold morning fog. The Celts gloried in such single combat and eagerly slaughtered vast numbers of terrified young Roman men. Here and there a few brave soldiers from the legions managed to rally and fight, but without hope for victory, only an honorable death as Roman soldiers. Many retreated into the water until they were up to their necks. Some tried to swim across the lake, but the distance was far too great and their heavy armor soon dragged them to death on the muddy bottom. Others fought in the water while the Numidian cavalry cut them down from atop their horses, including many who tried to surrender. A few begged their fellow Romans to kill them rather than face the Numidian swords.

Flaminius was horrified that he had marched his men into such a deadly trap, but he would not retreat and save himself. He could not survive the battle, but he faced his death with honor along with his men. Fifteen thousand Roman soldiers died that foggy summer morning at Lake Trasimene, with a few thousand more taken as prisoners. Hannibal had once again displayed an uncanny knack for using nature to his advantage in warfare. Only a small band of Roman veterans at the front of the line managed to fight their way out of the valley and into the hills above the lake. From there as the fog lifted they could see clearly the bloody slaughter and the awesome scale of the Roman loss. They escaped from the hills to a nearby Etruscan village where they were soon surrounded by Spanish cavalry. Such was their courage in the battle that Hannibal ordered them spared and taken prisoner. The Italians among them, like the other non-Roman prisoners from the battle, were once again pardoned and released to return to their homes without ransom.

Hannibal searched for the body of Flaminius to give him an honorable burial, but he was unable to locate it among the carnage. Like so many Roman soldiers that day, the general was likely slain and decapitated by one of the Celtic warriors who collected enemy heads as valued trophies, preserving them for years in cedar oil to show visitors. After the battle, the victorious Carthaginians walked through the mountains of bodies stripping them of their fine Roman weapons for their own use in future battles. Hannibal had lost perhaps two thousand of his own men, mostly Celts, in the conflict, showing that even in extreme circumstances the Romans were able to fight back against their enemies. But the staggering death toll suffered by the Romans at Lake Trasimene far outweighed the Carthaginian losses and secured for Hannibal one of the greatest and most terrible victories in the history of ancient warfare.

⊗

The situation quickly grew even worse for the Romans after the annihilation of Flaminius and his legions at Lake Trasimene. Servilius, the other consul for the year 217 B.C.E., was getting ready to head south from his camp at Arminium to meet Flaminius and face Hannibal together. He never imagined that his impetuous, outnumbered colleague would confront the Carthaginians alone. Servilius apparently hadn't heard yet about Flaminius's defeat and so sent four thousand cavalry soldiers as an advance guard into Tuscany. Servilius would soon follow with the rest of his army hoping to meet up with his fellow consul and defeat the Carthaginians before they could reach Rome.

Hannibal wasted no time glorying in victory but was planning his next move even before the crows had finished picking the bones clean at Trasimene. When he heard that the cavalry of Servilius was on the move,[2] he sent his trusted commander Maharbal north with his Numidian horsemen and light-armed javelin soldiers to surprise him. Maharbal caught the entire Roman force in Umbria and killed half of them immediately in a surprise attack, then took the remaining two thousand prisoner the next day after surrounding them on a nearby hill. It was an astonishing defeat for a well-prepared Roman cavalry force and immediately stopped Servilius from advancing with the rest of his army since without his horsemen he was both blind and unable to face Hannibal in open battle.

Rome had been thrown into a panic after the loss at Trebia the previous year, but the annihilation of their legions at Lake Trasimene and the defeat of Servilius's cavalry three days later shook them to their core. One consul was now dead and the other hiding behind the walls of his camp. It seemed certain that Hannibal and the entire Carthaginian army would soon fall on their city, a citadel that had not seen invaders at its gates in almost two hundred years. Walls were hastily repaired while thousands of farmers from the surrounding countryside flocked into the city with their families and animals. Mothers wept openly in the Forum for their slain sons and beseeched the gods at all the temples. Rumors of Carthaginian outrages swept across the city. Rome itself was now facing the kind of ruin and destruction they had so often meted out on their own enemies.

Religious dread was so widespread in the city that the Romans revived an archaic rite called the *lectisternium* designed to appease the gods. It had last been done two centuries earlier for only six gods and involved publicly dressing up statues of divinities and placing them on a couch (*lectus*) for a grand feast. This time matters were so dire that the Romans brought out images of all twelve Olympian gods for the sacred meal in hope of winning their favor. It was said in the streets that Flaminius had willfully neglected the traditional omens and rites before the battle at Trasimene. The Romans were now determined to invoke the whole pantheon of heaven.

But, as grim as their future seemed, no one among the senators or people ever considered surrendering the city. To do so would be to submit themselves to death or slavery—the same fate they themselves had inflicted on so many conquered people. They were determined to fight to the last man, woman, and child for their lives and freedom. The only question on the minds of the Romans was who could lead them now in their desperate fight against Hannibal.

CAMPANIA

The Romans hated the idea of a king and had designed their republican government to limit the power any one person might hold over them. Two independent consuls always shared chief executive authority for a year each. Nonetheless, even the freedom-loving Romans recognized there were times of extraordinary threat to the nation when they needed a single leader with unlimited power. This was the office of the dictator ("one who speaks"). If there was ever a time when such a man was needed, it was now.

Many ambitious senators might have thirsted for such power, but there was only one man the Roman people would trust with the awesome *imperium* to make his own word law. This was Quintus Fabius Maximus, a senator in his late fifties who had twice served Rome faithfully as consul. He was a proven commander in war who had defeated the wild Ligurians of northern Italy fifteen years earlier, but he was also a cautious general who would not lead the legions into foolish battles for his own glory. Fabius came from a distinguished family of the ancient Roman nobility and had no need to prove his worth to his country anew. He was steady and utterly loyal to the ideals and traditions of the Republic. Some might have questioned his selection as dictator because of his well-known hesitancy, but most, at least at the beginning, saw this quality as a valued attribute in a time of crisis. He also had some familiarity with the Carthaginians as he had traveled to Africa two years earlier as part of the Roman delegation when Hannibal had threatened Saguntum in Spain. At that time, when many in the Roman Senate were pushing for an immediate declaration of war on Carthage, Fabius had urged patience.

An officer known as the *magister equitum,* or "master of the horse," always served as second in command to a Roman dictator. To balance the caution of Fabius, the senate chose a younger man named Marcus Minucius Rufus for the job. Whereas Fabius was careful and conservative, Minucius was eager and innovative, perhaps even rash. He was also a political opponent of Fabius who many suspected would do everything possible to cause trouble for his new commander.

❧

Fabius immediately set to work recruiting thousands of fresh troops to fight Hannibal. Again the Roman advantage of a virtually inexhaustible supply of young men was evident as the dictator quickly raised a new army of forty thousand soldiers. Many of these were young lads from the ruined farms of central Italy who had a deep sense of patriotism and whose families took great personal offence at Hannibal's scorched-earth policy of burning their crops and homes. Fabius needed time to train them, but opted to have them learn on the march as Hannibal was too much of an immediate threat to spend months drilling in camps near Rome.

Contrary to what the Romans feared, Hannibal did not turn south and make for their city walls after his victory at Trasimene. The Carthaginian general knew the city was too strong and that he still didn't have enough men for a months-long frontal assault. He had to recruit more allies before he could consider storming the gates of Rome, so instead of heading south he led his army east through Umbria to the Adriatic Sea in the region of Picenum. From there, as summer turned into autumn, he made a slow march south down the coast seizing supplies and burning farms along the way. The farther Hannibal went from Rome, the more of a balancing act his policy of rural destruction became. He needed to feed his army and deny supplies to the Romans, but he was also eager to recruit Italian allies, who did not appreciate having their homes and livelihoods destroyed. He wisely focused his raiding and devastation on Roman colonies and their most loyal allies. His selective targeting seemed to have worked since his numbers of Italian soldiers steadily grew. He even managed to draw a few soldiers from the Etruscans who had long been Roman allies. On one tombstone carved in the Etruscan language many decades after the war, a very elderly man brags that the greatest glory of his life was to serve with the Carthaginian invaders:

Felsnas, son of Larth Lethe, lived at Capua and died at 106 years of age. He fought in the army of Hannibal.[1]

Wherever they came from, Hannibal took great care to see to the needs of his soldiers[2] as they moved down the coast. The pace was deliberately slow to rest his men from the trials of the past and to build their strength for what lay ahead. He was also concerned for his animals, especially his essential cavalry horses. Many of the mounts had developed mange during the months of hard travel, so that Hannibal employed a successful Carthaginian treatment of bathing them in old wine.

Hannibal's arrival at the Adriatic was also the first time since he had crossed into Italy a year earlier that he had direct access to the sea and could send messengers to Carthage by ship. The Carthaginians had heard of Hannibal's victories in Italy by that point and most were thrilled at the successes of their young general. But because of Roman superiority at sea, they sent word that they could regretfully offer little in the way of support or supplies. Even in the wake of Hannibal's conquests in the heart of their enemy's empire, the Carthaginian opposition leader Hanno was still doing everything he could to thwart the Barca family. Hannibal would remain on his own in Italy.

When his army had rested and was done plundering Roman properties in Picenum, Hannibal moved his army down the coast to the region of Apulia in Italy's boot. This was rich farmland with plenty of food for his hungry army. For many weeks, there were no Roman forces to challenge him, giving him complete reign over the countryside and a chance to build up his army with new Italian recruits. But then Fabius and his army arrived and made camp near the Carthaginian forces. The intelligence he had collected on the dictator indicated he would not be easily provoked. This presented a different kind of a challenge to Hannibal, who badly needed decisive battles to wear down the legions and to keep his Italian and Celtic allies rewarded with Roman spoils. The worst situation for Hannibal in Italy was a drawn-out war of attrition waged by a Roman commander who refused to face him with his full army.

Hannibal was a general who took risks and dared the unconventional. Now in Fabius he met a man who was the exact opposite.

Near the town of Arpi in northern Apulia, Hannibal decided it was time to test Fabius. He assembled his whole army in battle formation outside of the Roman camp and taunted the dictator to come out and fight if he dared. The soldiers of Fabius were eager for revenge against the Carthaginians for the slaughter of their comrades at Trasimene, but Fabius refused to move. His men all stood on the walls of their fort and watched Hannibal's army until the sun began to set, then the Carthaginians returned to their own camp for the night. This was Hannibal's first taste of how things were going to be different with a new commander.

The strategy of Fabius was sound but deeply unpopular with the Romans both among the soldiers and in the capital. Caution was one thing, but outright refusal to fight? It was simply un-Roman. But Fabius knew that Hannibal's forces were hardened troops who would easily defeat his own inexperienced soldiers in open battle. More importantly, he had no cavalry that could begin to match the skilled horsemen of Hannibal. Fabius's second-in-command, Minucius, was beside himself with frustration at the dictator's hesitancy. Instead of taking offensive action, Fabius ordered the Italian towns and farms in Hannibal's path to evacuate to safer areas and destroy their crops to keep them out of the Carthaginians' hands. As the weeks wore on, he continued to follow Hannibal at a distance, always keeping to the safe high ground and picking off the occasional enemy patrol. Because of this, Fabius soon gained the derogatory nickname *Cunctator* ("Delayer").

Unpopular as it was among the Romans, Fabius's plan held great promise—if only the indignant Romans would permit him to carry it out. Fabius's strategy allowed the Romans to take advantage of being on their home territory in Italy, while Hannibal was forced to rely on Italians he did not know well or necessarily trust for geographical information. Fabius could also draw on a virtually endless supply of soldiers while Hannibal was forever trying to woo, cajole, or bully new Italian allies into joining his army. In the long term, the Carthaginians were far more vulnerable in an extended war than the Romans were. If allowed time, Fabius could eventually wear down Hannibal. This strategy also allowed Fabius to train his soldiers and accustom them gradually to the Carthaginians without the risk of open battle. Finally, and perhaps most importantly, Fabius was taking the initiative in the war away from Hannibal. If the Romans would not be drawn into battle, the Carthaginian commander was forced into an endless and ultimately self-defeating conflict of raids and guerilla strikes in a foreign land. It was a fine life for brigands and pirates, but not for an army that needed impressive victories. His Italian allies and even his own men would soon lose heart if they couldn't face and defeat the Romans in decisive battles.

Hannibal needed a new strategy to respond to Fabius, so he began by moving his army from the shores of the Adriatic west across the mountains into the land of Campania[3] around the Bay of Naples. This land, known as the *Ager Falernus*, with its rich volcanic soil, was the heart of Roman agricultural production—and not coincidentally the favored area for the vast rural estates of wealthy Roman senators. Rome had seized much of the area over a century earlier, but the land was still a mosaic of peoples from different ethnic groups with deep roots in the local soil. Greek settlers had arrived five hundred years earlier and mixed amicably with the native Italians around port towns like Pompeii. It was only with the relatively recent confiscation of farms by Roman colonists that the natives had begun to lose control of their homeland. There was a great deal of anger against Rome among the fiercely independent people of

Campania, but they had enough experience with the legions not to lightly take up arms against Rome. They might be sympathetic, but Hannibal would have to prove he could defeat the Romans soundly before they would change sides.

Campania was shaped like a huge amphitheater with steep mountains on three sides and the sea to the west, while Mount Vesuvius loomed over the middle. Hannibal began in the east and started burning Roman farms as he moved toward the western sea. The Romans could either face him in battle or show the world that they had effectively surrendered their richest territory to Carthage. He could easily gather far more food than even his growing army needed as he moved around the plain daring the Romans to challenge him. He made a point of gathering intelligence about which estates belonged to the Roman elite and focused his destruction there—though he conspicuously left the farmlands owned by Fabius untouched. This was a move guaranteed to stir rumors among the senate that Fabius had made a secret deal with Hannibal to spare his estates in return for not engaging the Carthaginians in battle. Fabius's reputation was such that few believed such treachery could be true, but the seed was planted. Fabius was so horrified at the slur on his character that he ordered his farms in Campania sold to raise money to ransom Roman prisoners.

Still, Fabius continued his strategy of nonengagement with Hannibal. He kept to the rocky hills where Hannibal's cavalry could not operate and shadowed the Carthaginians as they moved around Campania. No one among the Romans was more outraged at Fabius's continuing inaction than his second-in-command Minucius, who was beside himself with rage:

> Have we come here as spectators to watch our allies being butchered and their property burned?[4]

Minucius ironically thanked Fabius for at least providing the Roman troops in the hills with such splendid seats for watching Italy laid waste. Rome was on the verge of revoking his dictatorship unless he did something soon to challenge the Carthaginians—but Fabius was firm. He would not face the superior enemy in open battle and risking another massive defeat like Trasimene. Hannibal had not succeeded in drawing Fabius out into battle, but he had turned the Romans against each other. His work in Campania that summer had gone very well indeed.

❧

As successful as Campania had been for Hannibal, it was also a trap. The steep mountains that surrounded the region had few passes that would allow the Carthaginians to escape back into Apulia for the winter. Fabius would not face Hannibal in open battle, but he welcomed the chance to attack the Carthaginians in a rocky, narrow pass where their superior cavalry would be useless. Fabius sent troops ahead to guard all the exits from Campania and followed the enemy forces closely waiting for his chance.

Hannibal was in a bind and knew that Fabius had a huge advantage if the Romans caught his soldiers on the mountain roads. Hannibal's best option for escape, probably via the Volturnus Valley north of Capua, was blocked by four thousand Roman troops who held the high ground. Nonetheless, Hannibal led his entire army to the entrance of the pass and made camp, while Fabius and his eager troops held a fortified hill above the valley. There was no way the Carthaginians could fight their way past the Romans without suffering tremendous losses. Even the cautious Fabius began to believe that he could end the war then and there.

Hannibal's solution to this dilemma[5] was inspired and typical of his unique ability to overcome a difficult situation through unconventional means. He ordered his army to gather as much dried wood as possible into small bundles. He then had his men herd together two thousand of the best oxen they had captured in Campania and tie the bundles of wood onto their horns along with twigs and dried vines. He selected a select group of infantry to station themselves around the oxen, then he ordered his men to eat a hearty supper and to rest so they could be ready for what he planned later that night.

There was a saddle in the hills between the Carthaginian and Roman camps and this was where the infantry drove the oxen when darkness fell. In the early hours after midnight when most of the Romans were asleep, Hannibal quietly roused his men and readied them to move up the main pass and through the mountains in the darkness. As for the oxen, he had the infantry herding them set fire to the bundles of wood on their horns and drive them up into the saddle over the hills. The Roman guards in the nearby pass saw what they thought were hundreds of torches carried by Carthaginian soldiers trying to escape through the saddle. They roused their comrades from sleep and sent word to Fabius, who refused to send the rest of his men out of their fortified camp since he believed it was one of Hannibal's traps. This was exactly what Hannibal thought Fabius would do. In darkness and general confusion, Hannibal's army then marched quickly through the lightly guarded pass with only minimal fighting and over the Apennines into Apulia with his men and treasure intact. Finally he sent some of his Spanish cavalry back through pass and attacked the unsuspecting Roman guards from the rear, allowing the infantry who had been driving the oxen to escape.

The imagination of Hannibal had once again triumphed over the Romans and made Fabius look foolish. Back in Rome, those who weren't weeping at the missed opportunity to destroy Hannibal were laughing at Fabius, with a grudging and growing admiration for the Carthaginian's ability to best them again and again in their own backyard. Minucius begged the senators to let him take over from his commander and face Hannibal in open battle. But, for the moment at least, Fabius still held the imperium. He ordered his troops to follow Hannibal back through the mountains into Apulia to wait for another day.

❧

The first and second years of Hannibal's invasion of Italy were filled with spectacular successes against the Romans. Though he did not win the outright victory in the war he might have hoped for, Hannibal established his reputation as a fearsome adversary and military genius. But the Romans were far from defeated and were wise enough not to make the war a purely Italian affair. Although their original plan to take the war to Africa had been abandoned, they maintained pressure on Carthage in Spain, cut off as it was from Hannibal's leadership.

Cornelius Scipio[6] had sent his brother Gnaeus from the Rhône to Spain with thousands of Roman troops just before Hannibal crossed the Alps. This may have hurt Cornelius in his subsequent conflicts with Hannibal, but it insured that the war would be fought on multiple fronts to Rome's long-term advantage. Gnaeus Scipio had reached Spain that autumn at the end of the fighting season and established his headquarters at Emporium on the northeast coast, a colony of Rome's faithful ally Massalia. Hannibal had left his lieutenant Hanno in Spain to guard the area between the Ebro River and the Pyrenees Mountains, though Hannibal's brother Hasdrubal Barca was the overall Carthaginian commander in Spain. Hanno was eager for his own victories and launched an attack on the Romans the next year near the coast. The Romans had never fought in Spain before, but they were able to soundly defeat and capture Hanno along with many of the valuable supplies that Hannibal had left in Spain. With this victory the Romans controlled the northeastern region of Spain and, for the time being, could block Hasdrubal from crossing into Italy and reenforcing his brother. With entry to Italy cut off, Rome could wage a more systematic war in Spain, gradually increasing their power in the peninsula while attempting to win the wavering Celts and Iberians to their side.

Hasdrubal was a Barca, however, and was not going to let the Romans take any of Iberia without a fight. He set out from New Carthage and crossed the Ebro where he found the sailors of Gnaeus Scipio's fleet ill-prepared for a surprise attack. Hasdrubal killed many of the Roman sailors at their shore defenses, while the remaining seamen fled to their ships for safety. Hasdrubal then built forts and bases nearby before retiring back to New Carthage for the winter. Gnaeus Scipio was furious when he arrived at the scene and turned his wrath on his own defeated sailors, who were beaten severely or executed for desertion of their posts.

The next spring Hasdrubal returned north of the Ebro River with his army and ships to face Gnaeus Scipio, but this time the Roman commander was ready. He met the smaller Carthaginian navy at the mouth of the Ebro and destroyed twenty-five of their ships. Hasdrubal was pushed back south of the river and the Roman navy took control of the seas east of Spain. They began to stage amphibious raids and assaults on Carthaginian forts and allies all along the coast, even to the south of New Carthage. The Romans also pressed the Balearic Islands until the inhabitants, allies of Carthage and source of the famed slingers of Hannibal's army, sued for peace. Gnaeus Scipio was so successful in Spain that the Roman Senate sent his brother to him with ships and supplies, and from that point on waged war together against the Carthaginians in Spain. The Barca family was far from defeated in Spain and had considerable resources left to fight the Romans there, but the success of the Scipios guaranteed that Hannibal was cut off from help from Iberia and would face whatever Rome had in store for him unaided.

GERONIUM

Hannibal's pressing concern as winter approached was to find a safe and suitable camp for his army in Apulia. He needed a well-fortified headquarters, preferably a walled town, with plenty of space and enough supplies and foraging in the nearby country-side for his tens of thousands of men. No army, not even Hannibal's after his successful raid in fertile Campania, could carry enough food with them to last for endless months. They needed pasturage and farms close at hand for the winter.

The Carthaginian commander settled on the town of Geronium[1] in northern Apulia, about 150 miles from Rome. It was far enough away from the capital to give Hannibal piece of mind but also close enough to make the Romans nervous. It also had abundant grain stored within its walls. Polybius says Hannibal sent a message to the citizens of Geronium offering an alliance and pledging his good will, but the people rejected his offer and were put to the sword after a brief siege. Livy, in contrast, says that the citizens had already abandoned the town before the arrival of Hannibal, who used their empty houses to store grain. Given that Livy rarely misses a chance to make Hannibal look bad, it's tempting to prefer his more temperate account.

Immediately after Hannibal escaped from Campania, Fabius returned to Rome temporarily. Some sources say it was to conduct necessary religious rituals, but more likely he was recalled to face hard questions from the senate. The people of Rome and even his own soldiers had taken to calling him the *paedagogus* of Hannibal. This was a derogatory Greek term for an old slave who followed a young boy to school carrying his books. The ever-cautious Fabius left his second-in-command Minucius in charge in the south and admonished him firmly to continue shadowing the Carthaginians but not to engage Hannibal. For the eager Minucius, however, this was an opportunity for action he was not going to miss.

Hannibal's main strength was his cavalry, so above all else he devoted himself to taking care of his horses. The pasture lands around Geronium were plentiful and rich with good Italian grass, but insuring that the horses could graze outside the walls of the town also put his men and animals at risk. To counter any threat from the legions, Hannibal established a small, fortified camp[2] on one of the hills in front of the town near the grasslands and close to the Roman camp to act as a deterrent against any Roman attack on his horses or foragers. In addition to those soldiers manning the hill fort, Hannibal also had a significant percentage of his army outside the city at any given time searching for supplies in the countryside. Minucius[3] carefully observed all these movements and decided now was his chance for glory.

On a day when the Carthaginian forces were spread most thin, the temporary Roman commander personally led his cavalry and fastest infantry troops out of their camp and fell on the enemy soldiers occupying the hill in front of the town. The Romans had received orders from Minucius that morning to show no mercy to the Carthaginians and take no prisoners. So many of Hannibal's men were out foraging that day that he lacked the manpower to march out of the town and counter the Roman strike. All he could do was stand on the walls of Geronium and watch. Minucius took the small camp on the hill and killed many of Hannibal's men. The surviving Carthaginians fled back inside the walls of the town.

The attack at Geronium was one of the few times in the whole Italian campaign that Hannibal was caught at a disadvantage. But to be fair, he had no choice. To feed his army and horses he had to send them out into the countryside to forage for food, leaving his small camp on the hill exposed. A more skeptical observer might wonder if even in this Hannibal knew exactly what he was doing.

Although Hannibal had lost some of his men and a little of his sheen of invincibility, the defeat was a relatively minor affair. The people of Rome, however, so desperate for good news, treated Minucius's victory as one of the greatest triumphs in the history of warfare. They proclaimed Minucius as their savior and forced the senate to appoint him as full co-commander with Fabius in the war. Surely now their young general would face Hannibal in traditional open battle and crush the Carthaginians into the dust, as Roman armies should. The humiliated Fabius returned to Apulia, having been forced to give half his troops to Minucius, who set up a nearby, separate camp from the dictator. He was not going to submit himself to Fabius's authority any longer. From now on, the glory of defeating the Carthaginians would be his alone.

As always, Hannibal was closely observing everything that happened on the Roman side. He could see with his own eyes that their army was now divided into two camps, one commanded by Fabius and the other by Minucius. His spies in the Roman camp reported to him that after his recent victory, the younger co-commander was more eager than ever to engage the Carthaginians and more confident that he alone could crush them. Not one to pass up such an opportunity, Hannibal laid his trap carefully. Between Hannibal's headquarters at Geronium and the camp of Minucius was a hill that was a strong and logical position for an advanced Carthaginian outpost. The hill itself was treeless and offered little obvious cover, but as Hannibal had discovered in his many rides around the area, it was filled with countless hollows that were not visible from the Roman camp. Under cover of darkness, Hannibal sent a large contingent of troops to hide in those depressions and wait there quietly until the next day. When morning came, he led his light infantry to the hill under the full view of the Romans. Minucius took great offense that Hannibal would dare to establish a post so close to his camp after the thrashing he had recently given the Carthaginians. He ordered his own light infantry and cavalry to advance to the hill immediately without waiting for heavy infantry support, then himself led the slower foot soldiers out of camp to the attack. He didn't bother to inform Fabius of his intensions since he had no desire to share the glory.

Hannibal's troops, operating from a higher position, were able to push back the advancing Roman infantry and their cavalry, whose horses were at a severe disadvantage moving on a rocky hill. Both Roman groups began to retreat back down the hill and promptly ran into the legions that Minucius was marching up to the top, throwing everything into confusion. At this opportune moment, Hannibal gave the signal for his thousands of troops concealed on the hill to spring out of their hollows and attack Minucius on all sides. The Roman general and his entire army were completely surrounded. What Minucius hoped would be a glorious victory swiftly turned into a desperate fight for survival. It was only the prompt arrival of troops sent by Fabius—who had been watching the whole debacle unfold—that rescued the situation from becoming another Trasimene. With the help of Fabius's veteran soldiers, the Romans were able to save Minucius and push back the Carthaginians, but with heavy losses to their legions. Hannibal then wisely withdrew his troops with minimal casualties, rather than face the combined Roman army in a hilly setting where he could not use his superior cavalry.

The reputation that Minucius had gained in his first victory over Hannibal was shattered in the second encounter. He was again reduced to second-in-command under Fabius. But with the autumn of 217 B.C.E. drawing to a close, the dictatorship of Fabius and the service of Minucius were due to expire at the end of December in any case, so both were recalled to Rome. The armies on both sides retired to their winter quarters as the season for battle ended, with temporary commanders sent from Rome to govern the army in camp. In January, a new pair of Roman consuls would be elected, but they would not take office until March. Fabius continued to defend his strategy of delay and nonconfrontation with Hannibal to the senate and people of Rome, but no one was in the mood to listen. Minucius may have been a disappointment, but Fabius was viewed as timid at best and at worst unfit to lead the legions of Rome against the Carthaginians. It would now fall on bolder men to rally the Republic against the dire threat of Hannibal.

❦

The mood in Rome was as black as it had ever been. Almost every battle against Hannibal over the last two years had ended in defeat and the death of tens of thousands of Roman soldiers. No family in Rome was left untouched by the loss of beloved fathers, sons, and brothers. As for strategy, both aggressive action and defensive warfare had failed against the Carthaginians. Hannibal had free reign over the countryside of Italy with more allies going over to his side each month. Paranoia flourished among the Romans, who saw conspiracies and evil omens everywhere. Twenty-five slaves were hastily crucified[4] on the Campus Martius just outside Rome for supposed collaboration with the enemy. Blood was reported to have flowed from statues and stones again fallen from the sky. Rome was filled with dread that the next summer Hannibal would at last march on the city and kill them all.

At the Carthaginian camp at Geronium, life continued with foraging for supplies and only minor skirmishes with the Romans as they waited for spring. Hannibal passed the cold months of the year wooing Italian allies and seeing to the myriad administrative details in governing what was essentially a city on the move. He possessed a genius for fighting, but Hannibal had learned much from his father in Spain and was an excellent administrator as well. Finding food for his hungry troops was a constant concern even with the stores they had at Geronium, as was keeping the men occupied. Prostitutes and camp wives made themselves at home among the men, as did merchants, vendors, and every manner of shopkeeper and entertainer offering their services for inflated prices. To pay his men, Hannibal even minted his own coins. The winter was free from battles, but the Carthaginian commander had no rest as he prepared for the coming summer.

In Rome, the newly elected consuls were Lucius Aemilius Paulus and Gaius Terentius Varro. Like Fabius, Aemilius Paulus was a member of one of the oldest and most distinguished patrician families of Rome. He was a proven leader and experienced general who just a few years before had defeated the fierce Illyrians across the Adriatic. Now at nearly sixty, he was ready to put all his talents to use one final time for his family's honor and for the Republic. Varro, on the other hand, was another new man who had fought his way to the highest ranks of the state. Livy disparages him, perhaps unfairly, as a crude social climber whose lowly father had owned a butcher's stall. Varro was also known as arrogant and impetuous, but without noble blood. Rome had once again elected two leaders who were complete opposites and unlikely to work together against the Carthaginians. Hannibal was already calculating how to best take advantage of this division between the consuls.

Aemilius Paullus and Varro spent the spring recruiting and training what was to be the largest and most formidable army in Rome's history. Agents scoured the farms of Italy for young men who could work hard and take orders. If the recruits didn't quite meet the age requirement, no one was going to raise a fuss. Rome was determined to destroy Hannibal this year by sheer overwhelming force of numbers, if nothing else. The vast sea of men serving under the Roman standards that summer was truly impressive, with roughly eighty thousand men taking up their swords to fight the Carthaginians. But with so many veteran Roman soldiers dead, at least half of the new army were teenagers with no fighting experience beyond chasing the occasional wolf or bear away from the family chickens. Still, these young Romans were a tough and brave lot who spent months that spring and early summer in hard battle training. Even though most of Hannibal's army was made up of experienced troops, they were scarcely half the number of Rome's legions. Under the competent leadership of the senior consul Aemilius Paullus, the Roman threat to crush the Carthaginians was not an idle boast.

14

CANNAE

That winter Hannibal carefully considered his next move. An enormous Roman army was assembling to march on him when summer began, and it would have been foolish even for a general of his talent to think he could easily defeat it in open battle. And yet, an open battle in which he could use his superb cavalry was his only hope of holding the Romans at bay and winning over more Italian allies for the next stage of the war. Hannibal therefore had to use every possible advantage he could muster to provoke the Romans into a conflict in a place and time of his own choosing. Throughout the winter, he rode through the countryside of southern Italy looking for locations where he could fight. He studied intelligence reports and carefully questioned his spies to learn everything he could about Roman logistics, along with the temperament and disposition of the new enemy commanders. By early summer he knew what he would do.

Just a few days south of his winter headquarters at Geronium was the small but strategic town of Cannae near the Adriatic coast on the far side of the Aufidus River. The Romans had established a large grain depot there to collect and store food for their army from the surrounding territory. If Hannibal could take the town, the Carthaginians would not only have plenty of grain for themselves, but they could starve the Roman army and keep it from operating against them in Apulia. The capture of Cannae was almost guaranteed to force Rome to attack the Carthaginians to take back their food supply. Not only was the grain crucial for Hannibal, but the countryside around Cannae was a gently rolling coastal plain with plenty of room for his cavalry to maneuver. If he could force the much larger Roman army to fight him there in open battle, he might have a chance to win.

Hannibal led his men out of winter quarters at a rapid march to reach Cannae before the Romans suspected what he was about to do. When he arrived at the poorly defended town, he quickly took it and secured the priceless grain stores for his own army. Now it was simply a matter of waiting for the Romans to show up. It didn't take long for the panicked senate to send both new consuls south to Cannae with their full army to take back the town, even though their raw recruits needed more training.

Sometime late in the hot, dry month of July, Hannibal stood on a low hill near Cannae and saw the Roman army approaching from the north. The crops had all been harvested in Apulia, so that the fields were brown and empty. The dust cloud from eighty thousand approaching soldiers and horses made the legions visible long before Hannibal could see the glint of their armor in the blazing sun. Rarely in history had so many men been assembled together for the purpose of killing their enemy. Even Hannibal, accustomed as he was to a life of war, stood in awe to see such a force drawing near. His officers and men watched as well, knowing that the greatest army on earth was bearing done on them. It was only their absolute trust in their commander that offered them any hope for what lay ahead.

Still, there were so many Romans coming that even some of Hannibal's veteran soldiers were deeply afraid. One Carthaginian officer named Gisgo was standing near Hannibal when the Romans marched over the horizon. He couldn't help but comment that their numbers were astonishing. "Yes," Hannibal replied, "but you haven't noticed something even more astonishing." The Carthaginian asked the general what that might be. Hannibal smiled and answered: "Not one of them is named Gisgo." All the officers standing close by began to laugh so hard that they forgot their fear. The front line soldiers near them heard the laughter and were put at ease knowing that if their leaders could laugh, things might be alright. The story quickly spread throughout the frightened army, giving them all confidence in the face of such a terrible threat. Hannibal, a master of battle psychology, knew how to inspire his men.

⧉

The Roman political system dictated that the two consuls alternate the days that they commanded the army. As Hannibal knew that with a little bit of luck, this changing of leadership allowed him to choose which general he would engage on any given day. This lack of continuity was a serious weakness in Roman military operations and was built on a fear of giving one man too much power over the military. So fearful was Rome of a would-be king that they were hesitant to alter this custom even when their enemy was clearly well aware of it and ready to exploit it. When the legions arrived at the plains just north of the Aufidus River, Aemilius Paullus saw that the area was flat and treeless, perfect for Hannibal's cavalry. He told Varro that they were not going to engage the Carthaginians there, at least not while he was in command. Varro argued with his fellow consul and told him their superior numbers negated any advantage Hannibal might have with his horsemen, but the older man refused to budge.

The next day Varro took over leadership[1] of the legions, ordering the men to break camp and advance toward the Carthaginians. Hannibal knew that Varro was in charge that day and suddenly hit the marching Romans hard with his light infantry and cavalry. It was more of a skirmish than a battle, but Varro and his men fought hard all day against the Carthaginians and pushed them back—just as Hannibal had intended. Varro was now more confident than ever that he was the man to lead the Romans to glorious victory over Hannibal. When Paullus took over the next day, instead of fighting he had the men rapidly build two strong defensive camps, one on the north bank of the Aufidus and one on the south. The senior consul was still not pleased with the lay of the land, but he needed the captured grain and knew that Rome was demanding he put the massive army to use. The area south of the river was slightly better for battle in his estimate, so he reluctantly determined they that was where he would meet the Carthaginians—again, as Hannibal had intended. He couldn't change the fact that Varro would be in command the next day when the battle would clearly take place, but he could give the Romans every advantage. Hannibal matched Paullus and moved his camp to the south of the river where he could more easily use his Numidian cavalry to harass the Roman water bearers and keep the enemy thirsty in the hot summer sun.

That night Hannibal gathered his men[2] together in the cool of the evening to encourage them for the upcoming fight. He spoke to them of the advantages they held on the plain of Cannae even though they were far outnumbered by the Romans. Cannae, he assured them, was perfect ground for the cavalry who would protect them in battle. The Romans may have more infantry, he admitted, but Carthage has several thousand more skilled and experienced horsemen. He had also maneuvered the Romans to make their camp on the seaward side of the plain where the fierce, hot winds from his native Africa would blow in their faces as they advanced the next day. Their eyes would be blinded and their tongues soon parched as they fought against the Carthaginian front standing toward the sea. Finally, Hannibal told his men that if they would hold the line and follow his orders to the letter—even if his commands seemed unusual—they could win. Some of them would die, he admitted, but that is the nature of war. He then echoed a firm belief of the many Celts among them, that he who falls in battle will be born again after a short time.

At dawn the next morning, the Romans and Carthaginians lined up facing each other on the plain south of the river. Paullus was unhappy about the lay of the land but was forced to yield command to Varro that fateful day. The younger consul put his enormous heavy infantry[3] forces in the center of the line facing south and packed closely together to make them an impenetrable wall. He was determined that no Carthaginians would break the deep Roman line and that his men would advance unstoppable and crush the enemy beneath their overwhelming numbers. On the right side of his line near the river, under the command of Paullus, was the Roman citizen cavalry, loyal and brave men but not as skilled as their allies in fighting from horseback. On the left wing under his own command were the Celtic and other allied cavalry fighting for the Romans that day. The Roman battle line stretched well over a mile in length and was a terrifying eighty thousand men deep. Half of these were undertrained teenagers who had never seen war, but their numbers were so enormous that the sheer mass of the legions shook the earth when they marched. Varro had also wisely placed his citizen cavalry on the right side, up against the Aufidus River to prevent the Carthaginians from riding around their lines on the right and attacking them from behind. The Roman citizens and allied cavalry would defend the ends of the two lines while the heavy infantry would advance and break through the less numerous Carthaginians in the center. It was a good plan and was almost certain to work if they could keep the Carthaginian cavalry from flanking them. Even if the enemy horsemen somehow got through, how could the Carthaginians hope to defeat so many Roman soldiers? There was a crowd of Roman senators present among the command that morning at Cannae. The Roman elite were confident that this would be the day they would finally crush the Carthaginians and no one wanted to miss it.

Hannibal had played out all the possible battle scenarios in his mind many times so that he knew exactly what he would do as he watched the Romans line up. On his left by the river facing the Roman citizen cavalry he stationed his own Celtic and Iberian horsemen. On his right he placed his fierce Numidian cavalry to face the allied Roman horsemen. With he himself in command in the center of his line, he placed his Iberian and Celtic infantry, vastly outnumbered by the Romans but made up of experienced soldiers who had looked death in the eye many times. To help counter the Roman advantage in numbers, he positioned his foot soldiers not in a straight line, but arching slightly forward toward the Romans.

They may have been fewer in number, but the veteran Iberian and Celtic infantry were a terrifying sight to the young Roman recruits. The screaming Celts with their long hair and golden torcs stood a head above most of the Romans and fought in brightly colored clothing, often bare-chested in their bravado. The Carthaginian line was the same length as the Roman forces, but they were stretched painfully thin and thus vulnerable to being pushed back by the legions. If Varro could push hard enough, he could break through Hannibal's lines and divide the Carthaginians in two, leading to certain victory.

When the sun was high in the sky, the Roman trumpets finally sounded the attack. The Roman armored infantry in the frontmost wave were hit by missiles from Hannibal's Balearic sling men, but few of the infantry fell. Then the bulging center of Hannibal's line felt the full force of tens of thousands of Romans pushing relentlessly against them and stabbing them with their short but lethal swords. The Carthaginians slowly began to fall back under the relentless pressure of the Roman infantry.

On the sides of the line things were looking better for Hannibal. The Roman citizen cavalry had placed themselves hard against the river to keep the Carthaginian cavalry from riding around them, but this meant the Roman horsemen had no space to move. They were packed so tightly that many were forced to dismount and fight on the ground at a huge disadvantage. The Carthaginian cavalry were able to push the Roman horsemen back along the river until their line finally broke, exposing the whole right flank of the Roman army. On the Roman left, the Numidian cavalry ran through the allied Roman horsemen even more quickly and opened up the rear of the Roman line to attack from behind.

Meanwhile, the Carthaginian center was falling steadily back under the Roman infantry onslaught. None of the Roman leaders seemed to have suspected it, but this was exactly what Hannibal had planned. Just as he had done in earlier battles, his feint drew the Romans deep into the center of his army until they were surrounded and then attacked by Carthaginian cavalry from behind. Although the Romans far outnumbered the Carthaginian forces, they had no room to move and nowhere to run. The Romans were now cut off from cavalry support on both sides, with many of their allied horsemen hastily abandoning the field. Their commander Varro, so eager for a fight at the beginning of the day, had fled the battlefield as soon as the Roman left flank was overrun, leaving the army to fend for itself. His more steady colleague Paullus was wounded early in the fight but refused the offer of a horse to escape and was soon killed. On the dusty plains of Cannae, tens of thousands of Roman soldiers were cut down by Hannibal's men that day without mercy. Young Roman farm boys who had dreamed of glory were slaughtered like spring lambs as they cried out in vain to the gods for help. Roman senators, officers, centurions, and common soldiers alike all fell together in one of the most deadly and horrifying days of war in human history.

The Roman army was destroyed at Cannae. At dawn the next day when Hannibal and his officers surveyed the carnage,[4] even the most hardened among them were astonished at what they had done. The fighting between the Carthaginians and the surrounded Roman heavy infantry was savage by any measure. With so little room to move, many of the Romans had been stabbed with spear and sword attacks that left the young men mortally wounded with thighs and tendons slashed, but even now were still barely alive. Many bared their necks and begged any Carthaginian passing by to put them out of their misery. Some of the Roman dead were found with their heads buried in holes they had dug in the bloody ground in an attempt to suffocate themselves. The Romans had fought fiercely, nonetheless. One mutilated Numidian infantryman dragged barely alive from under a dead Roman said that the enemy soldier, unable to hold a sword any longer in his hands, had used the last of his strength to gnaw off the Numidian's nose and ears with his bare teeth.

Among the Roman dead, aside from Varro's co-commander Aemilius Paullus, were many former consuls, praetors, questors, tribunes, and over eighty senators. Former Master of the Horse Minucius, who had longed to be the one to defeat Hannibal, had died bravely on the battlefield as well, refusing to flee the Carthaginians. Varro had fled from the slaughter with barely fifty men, including the younger Scipio, who had loyally seen to the safety of his commander. Many of the allied Roman cavalry had been able to flee when the battle turned hopeless, but for the trapped foot soldiers there was no escape. The Carthaginians spared a few thousand as prisoners for future ransom, but the scale of Roman loss was incredible. The numbers are uncertain, but estimates of sixty thousand dead may not be far off the mark. Perhaps one in five Roman men of fighting age died that day at Cannae.

Hannibal had achieved one of the greatest battlefield victories in history, but his own losses were heavy enough to worry him. Although relatively few compared to the Romans, at least five thousand of his men, mostly Celtic allies, had perished. This was small compared to the cost he had inflicted on Rome, but as ever he was at a disadvantage for finding replacement soldiers for his ranks. It was, nonetheless, a day of rejoicing for the Carthaginians, who buried their dead and divided the spoils of battle among the common soldiers as a reward for their extraordinary valor on a day of war like no other.

15

ROME

There is a story[1] that after Hannibal's triumph at Cannae his officers crowded around to congratulate him on his stunning victory. Most of his lieutenants counseled rest for the army after such a heroic effort. But Maharbal, Hannibal's old friend and the commander of his cavalry, urged just the opposite. "Now is the time to strike and bring the war to an end," he declared. "Let me rush the cavalry to Rome while the city is defenseless. Bring the army behind me and in five days you can feast on the Capitoline Hill at the heart of Rome, your conquered enemy." Although Hannibal appreciated Maharbal's enthusiasm, the Carthaginian general demurred and said he must take time to carefully consider his next move. Maharbal shook his head and replied: "You know how to gain a victory, Hannibal, but you don't know how to use it."

For two thousand years, historians, with the luxury of hindsight, have debated whether or not Hannibal should have marched on

Rome after his overwhelming victory at Cannae. Even centuries later in imperial Rome, the subject was a favorite topic of debate among students of rhetoric. But if we accept that Hannibal was one of the greatest military leaders of all time, and if we believe he was not a man given to unnecessary hesitation, then we need to try to understand why he made his fateful decision to not attack Rome at the moment of its greatest weakness.

Hannibal, like every general in the ancient world, knew that to take a fortified city surrounded by high stone walls was much harder and took vastly more resources than defeating an enemy on an open battlefield. The technology to quickly breach a wall simply didn't exist in Hannibal's day and would not be invented for many centuries. The only viable option for conquering a fortified city in ancient times was to surround it, cut off its food supplies, and try to starve it out while the inhabitants rained down missiles and death onto your own army from its high walls. The ten-year siege of Troy by the invading Greek forces is probably legend, but the reality of its formidable defensive situation was not. Hannibal had learned firsthand at the smaller walled city of Saguntum that siege warfare was arduous and time-consuming. To attack and successfully take an enormous, well-defended city such as Rome was a task that would have consumed months, if not years. Not only would Hannibal need to organize and wage an assault against an enemy capital in the heart of hostile territory, but he would have to hold his allies focused on their task through endless, dreary months of siege. The fickle Celts, who made up a large part of his army, scarcely had the patience for such a campaign. Even the Italians he had gathered into his coalition would have been difficult to satisfy without the promise of frequent battle and plunder.

But the most important reason why Hannibal didn't attack Rome immediately after his victory at Cannae was that he did not expect it to be necessary. The complete and violent destruction of an enemy capital was rare in ancient warfare. A hostile army would usually invade an enemy's land, win a few battles, burn and loot the countryside, and then negotiate a settlement on favorable terms with their adversary. Total war was impractical and inefficient for both sides. Carthage itself had capitulated to Rome in their first war after the Romans had taken Sicily and threatened to invade Africa. The Carthaginian Senate came to terms with Rome while still preserving most of their lands and wealth, even after paying a heavy indemnity. The investment of time and resources needed for the complete annihilation of an enemy was simply too much for most nations to seriously consider.

The story of Hannibal's boyhood oath to his father to despise Rome forever did not mean he wanted to kill every man, woman, and child in the city and reduce their homes to rubble. Although he hated what Rome had done to his city and wanted to conquer them, Hannibal's ultimate goal was to restore the glory and power of Carthage to the days before the conflict with Rome began. Reasonable peace terms by any measure of the times would have meant a Roman withdrawal from all the territory the city had acquired in the last two centuries, including Sardinia, Corsica, and Sicily. Hannibal would have also insisted that the Romans abandon the Celtic territories of northern Italy and probably the Greek and native Italic lands in the south as well. Rome would have been reduced to a regional power in central Italy with no offensive navy or military ambitions beyond the hills of Latium. Carthage would have imposed large war indemnities on the city as well, much as they themselves had been forced to pay after the conquest of Sicily. But after the war was over, Rome would have remained free and the Romans themselves would have been able to live their lives in peace. Given the uncertainties and dangers of life in the ancient world, this would have been an end to the war that any reasonable nation would have accepted.

The problem was that Rome was not like other nations. When the Greek general Pyrrhus had invaded Italy decades before and beaten the Romans in battle time after time, they always regrouped and never asked for terms. Unlike almost every other city in the Mediterranean at the time, Rome never considered backing down. The Romans neither accepted mercy from nor granted it to their enemies. If there was any failing that Hannibal had as a general, it was that he didn't fully realize what kind of an opponent he was dealing with. He was operating by the established rules of ancient warfare, which were certainly harsh but didn't seek the utter desolation of a land and its people. Rome didn't care about these rules. One day in the not-too-distant future, the Romans would obliterate the city of Carthage, slaughter its people, and curse its ruins so that no one would live there again. That was how Rome played the game of war.

After the Battle of Cannae, Hannibal gathered all of his Roman prisoners[2] to address them, the first time in the war he had done so. Hannibal, a gifted student of languages, may well have known Latin and could have spoken to them directly. He told them that he was not seeking to destroy their city, but to negotiate a reasonable peace between Rome and Carthage. His own city had yielded to Rome in the past when defeated in war, but now circumstances had changed. If Rome would pay a modest ransom, they would all be released alive and well to return to their families. They could testify to their countrymen that Rome could survive and even prosper in a world in which they were a smaller but still a free and independent nation. Hannibal then told them to select ten spokesmen from among themselves to return immediately to Rome and present his terms to the Roman Senate. He asked only for their word that they would return to his camp when their task was done. He would send with them a Carthaginian nobleman named Carthalo to personally represent him before the leaders of Rome and hear their reply.

⚏

Rome was filled with panic after the news of the defeat at Cannae reached the gates. Women wept openly on every street, for no family in the city was untouched by the loss of someone much loved. The imminent festival of Ceres, the goddess of grain, which was organized by the city matrons, was canceled since women in mourning were forbidden to participate and therefore was no one left to celebrate the rites. Citizens began to gather their belongings to flee to the hills, expecting Hannibal and his savage barbarian army to arrive any moment. *Hannibal ad portas*— "Hannibal is at the gates"—was the cry sweeping the town. The senate immediately posted guards at all the gates, not to keep the Carthaginians out but to keep the people of the city from leaving. People believed the gods had truly abandoned them and blamed anyone they could think of. One Vestal Virgin[3] suspected of yielding her sacred chastity to an unscrupulous lover was buried alive as punishment, while her paramour was lashed to death. A Roman envoy named Fabius Pictor, later a key historian of the Punic Wars, was sent to the Greek temple at Delphi to consult the god Apollo for advice on what the city should do to defeat Carthage. The oracular Sibylline Books, opened only in times of greatest crisis, were carefully searched for a way to appease the gods. The surprising answer they gave was to kill a Celtic man and woman, along with a Greek man and woman, in the public cattle marketplace in an un-Roman act of human sacrifice. The citizens of the city were not at all squeamish about the shedding of blood, but such a barbaric ritual was exceedingly rare in Rome and shook even the most hard-hearted among them.

The Roman Senate immediately appointed a new dictator, Marcus Junius, with Tiberius Sempronius Gracchus as his Master of the Horse. The city badly needed troops since it had lost so many legions at Cannae. They began to recruit farm boys under sixteen years old into the army and even purchased eight thousand slaves on the open market to serve in the military. Promised their freedom if they survived what lay ahead, the slaves gladly agreed. But for Rome to buy slaves and arm them to fight alongside children illustrates the depths to which the Republic had sunk. To arm the troops, the senate pleaded for households to donate their old swords and spears, while antique weapons were stripped from the walls of temples. In this way, Rome quickly raised a new army of twenty-five thousand soldiers.

When Hannibal's envoy Carthalo arrived at the gates of Rome he was met by a lictor bearing the symbols of the new dictator. In the name of Marcus Junius and the people of Rome, Carthalo was ordered to depart the city by nightfall. He would receive no hearing from the senate nor would Hannibal's offered terms of surrender be considered. The ten Roman representatives captured at Cannae who accompanied Carthalo were told that neither they nor their fellow prisoners would be ransomed by the state. In addition, no private citizens would be allowed to pay for the release of their family members or friends with their own funds. There would be no ransom, no negotiation, no surrender.[4] Other cities and nations might yield to defeat, but Rome would fight against Hannibal and his army to the last man. The ten Romans understood and so, honoring their word, made their way back to Hannibal to face their fate.

CAPUA

With Hannibal's decision not to march on Rome and the refusal of the Romans to consider surrender, the war in Italy settled into a long period of Carthaginian occupation and steady success in recruiting both local and international allies. Hannibal's strategy of slowly winning over the Italians to his side proved increasingly fruitful as each year more Samnite, Greek, and other cities in Southern Italy cast in their lots with the Carthaginians. The Romans meanwhile returned to the proven Fabian strategy of shadowing Hannibal's army without engaging him in open battle.

As Hannibal grew stronger in Italy, Rome grew weaker. Foreign kings and rulers from around the Mediterranean who had scoffed at the Carthaginian chances of success when Hannibal first crossed the Alps now took notice and began to send envoys to his camps in Italy to forge alliances. No one wanted to be standing with the

Romans when Hannibal finally crushed them, as it now seemed certain he would do in time. If Rome was foolish enough not to follow the rules of ancient warfare and surrender when clearly beaten, the cities and nations from Syria and Greece to the Atlantic Ocean would shed no tears when Rome at last fell, their men were slaughtered, and their families sold into slavery. Everyone knew all too well the Roman belief in their own expansionist destiny and their methods of aggressive warfare. Although capable of conquest and bloodshed, the Carthaginians, with their established mercantile history and lack of imperialist ambitions, were much to be preferred.

With Rome having suffered so many defeats in Italy, Hannibal now sent his brother Mago as his envoy to speak directly to the people and leaders of Carthage. Many of the merchant princes of the city had been reluctant supporters if not outright opponents of the Barca family and their adventures in Spain. Even more saw the invasion of Italy as an unnecessary provocation of one of the most powerful nations in the world. But after Cannae, even those who had stood against Hannibal admitted he had accomplished something truly remarkable.

Rome still controlled the seas between Italy and Africa, so the Carthaginian ship that brought Mago home must have picked him up secretly somewhere along the southern Italian coast and slipped quietly across the Mediterranean to avoid Roman naval patrols. When he arrived at last in Carthage,[1] it was a joyous occasion for the city. Celebrations honored the returning hero and his famous brother. Mago addressed the Carthaginian Senate and related firsthand accounts of the victories in Italy. The battles at Ticinus, Trebia, Trasimene, and of course Cannae, were all recited in glowing terms by a man who had been there to see the Romans fall. Not a vain man, Mago gave all the credit to his brilliant brother and listed the Roman generals, consuls, and dictators that Hannibal had bested. Over two hundred thousand Roman soldiers lay dead at his brother's hands and fifty thousand prisoners had been captured. The Celts of the north and many of the Italian cities of the south had joined the Carthaginian cause to defeat the Romans and destroy their ravenous empire. The gods themselves had clearly sided with Carthage against the might of Rome. Then, with a fine theatrical flair, Mago ordered the collected gold rings of the slain Roman *equites*, or knights, the heart of the Roman military leadership, to be poured on the floor of the Carthaginian Senate house. The mound of shimmering golden rings rose high and impressed even the most reluctant of the merchant princes of the city.

Mago then addressed the most important reason he had made the long journey to Africa. He said that although the war in Italy was going well, it was being fought far from the safety and resources of Carthage. By necessity, Hannibal was using an enormous amount of grain and money each month to feed and maintain the army, but was restrained from ransacking the southern Italian countryside for food by his need to recruit allies from the local people. What the Carthaginian army needed more than anything was food, cash, and new recruits to fill their ranks.

A loud cry of joyous support rose from the leaders and people of the city. When at last the shouting had died down, one man stood alone and to address those gathered there. To no one's surprise, it was Hanno, the longtime implacable opponent of the Barca family. Not swayed by stories of military victory or treasures brought from Italy, he pointedly asked Mago if the Romans had yet sent ambassadors to Hannibal's camp to sue for peace? If not, it hardly seemed like the war was a success to him. But the voice of Hanno was quickly drowned out by the crowds gathered that day. The people's assembly issued a decree immediately authorizing four thousand fresh Numidian cavalry for Hannibal, along with forty elephants and plentiful silver. They also approved Mago's own request to travel directly to Spain and recruit twenty thousand more Iberian infantry and four thousand additional cavalry. As Mago sailed away from Carthage, he was certain that his brother would soon have even more troops on the ground in Italy that could hopefully bring an end to the war and finally crush the Romans.

⊗⊗

M eanwhile, across the sea Hannibal was struggling to woo more cities to his side. He was largely successful in the months after Cannae and able to peel away important communities that had long been attached to Rome, but his victories in recruiting allies were far from universal. Many of the cities of southern Italy were controlled by ruling families with close business and marriage ties to Rome. Though they had no great affection for their masters on the Tiber River, they were all too familiar with the might and endurance of the Romans. In addition, their control over the lower classes in their own towns often depended on support from Rome, making them reluctant to switch sides and risk losing their own power. They admitted that the Carthaginians were impressive, but how could they believe that in the long term they would be better allies than the Romans, who were at least the devil they knew. In many cases Hannibal's ability to win over an Italian city depended on his appeal to the merchant class and commoners of a town who were more willing to give the Carthaginians a chance.

The prize Hannibal sought most of all was the large and important commercial city of Capua,[2] a day's march north of Naples. The

Carthaginian leader had long desired the port city of Naples itself, but was unable to pry it loose from Rome by diplomacy and rejected the idea of the long siege needed to take the town. Still, if he could win over Capua he would have an even larger, wealthier, and more important city to use as a base in Campania. The elite of the town hesitated because of their close ties to Rome, but many of the city's businessmen and working-class people had long resented Rome as an upstart newcomer in the Italian power game. The Capuans traced their roots back to the earliest Greek settlers in Italy, though they were now dominated by Samnites who spoke Oscan, not Latin, in the marketplaces and at home. The Romans had granted them some legal protections and limited control of their own local affairs, but the Capuans were not allowed full Roman citizenship and so could not vote or run for office in Rome. This second-class citizenship did not sit well with a city that saw itself, not Rome, as the rightful leading power in Italy. Many citizens of the town argued that Hannibal's victories provided the perfect opportunity to restore the proper order in Campania and beyond. A treaty now with the Carthaginians would cost little since Rome was in dire straits. When the war was finished and the victorious Hannibal sailed back to Africa, Capua would be left to consolidate its power in Italy.

When Hannibal marched back into Campania following Cannae, an official Capuan delegation approached him to negotiate terms of an alliance. Hannibal was thrilled to win over such an important ally and granted many generous concessions to the city in exchange for their loyalty. He agreed that the Carthaginians would have no authority over its citizens and that no Capuan would be compelled to fight or perform any service for Carthage against his will. In short, the city would regain its independence lost to Rome many years before in exchange for joining a loose coalition with the Carthaginians.

Although the defection of Capua was more of a symbolic than practical victory for Carthage, it was a devastating psychic blow to the Romans. Capua was the greatest and most important city of Italy after Rome and was the strategic and commercial center of Campania. It was also a long-time ally that the Romans believed they had treated graciously as a junior, though naturally inferior, partner in their growing empire. The Romans now raged against the Capuans and decried them as arrogant, unworthy traitors who would someday pay the price for their perfidy. The Capuans smiled and shrugged, then rounded up and locked away any remaining Roman citizens in the public baths, where they were deliberately asphyxiated in the heat. Soon after, Hannibal marched into Capua as a welcome guest and hero at the head of his army. He was cheered by adoring crowds in the streets and then addressed the Capuan Senate, thanking them for their friendship and promising they would not regret their decision.

But not everything went well for Hannibal in the years after Cannae. Soon after winning over Capua, the Carthaginian general moved into southern Campania to win over the reluctant city of Nola.[3] The people of the town were divided as to whose side they should choose, so the pro-Roman party in the city sent word to the nearby Roman praetor Marcus Claudius Marcellus that they needed reinforcement immediately or would be compelled to join Hannibal's cause. Marcellus, an experienced war leader, roused his army and marched to Nola by backroads through the mountains to avoid Hannibal's army. The Carthaginians had briefly left the region of Nola to attack a nearby city, so Marcellus was able to enter the town and close the gates behind him. When Hannibal returned, the two sides skirmished several times before the walls, but Marcellus was wise enough not to accept his repeated invitations to an open battle on Carthaginian terms. The people of

Nola, however, were growing very nervous with the legendary Hannibal just outside their gates and were preparing to surrender the city. Marcellus knew he had to take a risk or lose the town. The next time Hannibal drew his forces up before the walls as an invitation to fight, Marcellus ignored him just long enough to convince the Carthaginian leader he would not be engaging him that day. Then when Hannibal ordered his men to turn around and return to camp, Marcellus, in a masterpiece of timing, rushed from the gates and hit the enemy from behind with his full force. Hannibal was uncharacteristically caught off guard and lost several thousand soldiers that day. He then withdrew from Nola and shifted his efforts elsewhere in Campania. After the battle, celebrated as a great victory in Rome, Marcellus promptly beheaded seventy men from Nola that he deemed insufficiently loyal to the Romans as an example to the rest of Italy.

And so the drawn-out war of the Carthaginians and Romans continued in southern Italy as the years passed by. Hannibal won new alliances with foreign powers such as Philip V of Macedon and supported a successful though short-lived rebellion on the island of Sardinia. Celtic allies in northern Italy continued their own fight against Rome and on occasion defeated the legions there. The great city of Syracuse in Sicily, so often at odds with Carthage in the past, switched sides and for a short time provided Carthage an important new ally positioned strategically between Italy and Africa. Then three years after Cannae, Hannibal took the large Italian city of Tarentum after some leading citizens smuggled in Carthaginian forces, led by Hannibal himself, to attack the Romans stationed there. Although the Romans managed to hang on to the citadel in the city harbor, Hannibal gained a key Italian port.

The Romans however had learned many valuable lessons in their war with Hannibal. While using Fabian tactics (and Fabius himself) to contain the Carthaginians in southern Italy, they prudently looked beyond the Italian peninsula for how they might ultimately defeat Carthage. They realized Sicily was the key strategic location and so redoubled their efforts to regain control of the whole island, beginning with taking Syracuse back. A mighty Athenian armada had failed to seize the fortified city in an ill-fated assault during the Peloponnesian War two centuries earlier, so the Romans knew it would be no easy task. But even the generals of the Roman legions couldn't have expected the unlikely tactics they faced. The Greek scientist Archimedes,[4] a native of Syracuse, was in Syracuse during the attack and turned his extraordinary scientific talents to defeating the Romans. He constructed machines to counter the Roman siege engines and negate their advantages. His enormous catapults launched giant missiles that sank Roman ships in the harbor. He also invented cranes that could lift any enemy ship that strayed too close straight out of the water and disable it. A large parabolic mirror of his own devising focused the rays of the sun on Roman ships so that they burst into flame. For two years Archimedes and his mechanical wonders held the invaders back from taking Syracuse, so that soon the Romans began believing they were facing a supernatural enemy. But in time, by maintaining a safe distance from the walls and starving the city with a blockade, the Romans were able to storm the town and win it back from Carthage. One story says that at the end Archimedes was tracing mathematical equations in the sand when a young Roman soldier, not knowing who he was, ran him through with a spear.

The Romans then turned their attentions to retaking Capua. The legions besieged the city but could not force its surrender. Hannibal in turn attacked the Roman army as it surrounded the town but was unable to drive them off. The fight for the greatest city of southern

Italy soon became a stalemate that Hannibal could not afford. The resources required to relieve Capua were taxing his supplies on a massive scale, as the Romans had intended. Faced with an unwinnable situation at the leading town in Campania, Hannibal devised a bold ploy to draw the legions away from Capua—he decided to attack Rome itself.[5]

It had been five years since his victory at Cannae when Hannibal at last decided to lead his army to the gates of the enemy's capital. True to form he kept his campfires burning the first night before Capua to make the enemy think he was still nearby, but soon everyone knew the Carthaginians were on their way north. In fact, Hannibal wanted his presence known. He looted and burned farms all along the way to create a sense of panic—*Hannibal was coming*. Farmers began pouring into Rome, taxing the resources of the city. Women once again ran to the shines of the gods to beg heaven's help against the barbarians approaching at the gates. Fabius Maximus, the great delayer, told the city that Hannibal was just using the march to relieve pressure on Capua, but many of the common people would not listen to his voice of reason. The parents of Rome had long told their naughty children that Hannibal would come and snatch them from their beds if they didn't behave. Now it looked like he really would.

The Roman generals at Capua divided their forces in two with half rushing back to protect their home city, just beating the Carthaginians to the walls. Hannibal himself made camp just a few miles outside of town. He then led a troop of two thousand cavalry to the Porta Collina gate on the northern side of the city. There was a temple of Hercules near this spot where Hannibal sacrificed to his patron deity in full view of the Romans on the walls. As ever, Hannibal was a master of psychological warfare, invoking the favor of his favorite god at the Roman's own temple.

For Hannibal, it was the first time in all his years in Italy that he had seen the great city of his enemy for himself. With great bravado he rode along the miles of city walls just out of spear range, examining the defenses. For most Romans, it was the first time they had seen the great man for themselves. Before their own eyes was the dreaded general who had crossed the Alps and had killed almost a quarter million of their own soldiers. But despite their fear, they still would not yield. When the Roman owner of the land Hannibal was camped on announced that the occupied fields were for sale, buyers eagerly bid full price with a defiant eye to the future.

Back in Capua, the besieged citizens believed they had been deserted by Hannibal and lost all hope. The city's senate met and determined to surrender to the Romans, hoping for mercy. Almost thirty of the Capuan elders were wise enough to realize they would find no such clemency and poisoned themselves before the gates were opened to the legions. Many others wished they had done so after the Romans marched in. Seventy of the surviving Capuan senators were executed and many of the nobles were taken prisoner. Most of the citizens of the city, including the women and children, were sold into slavery to live out their lives in servitude far from home. The city's rich farmland was divided among Roman investors and any remnant of freedom in the greatest town of Campania vanished forever. Rome did not forgive and it never forgot.

It had seemed Hannibal's plan to march on Rome would be an effective tactic to draw at least a part of the Roman army away from his ally and give Capua a chance to shake off the Roman siege. He even managed to create a very real sense of panic among many of the citizens of Rome. But Hannibal knew even before the march began that he no longer had the manpower or resources to take the city. Even Hannibal's admirers couldn't help but wonder if there was an element of frustrated recklessness in the Carthaginian leader's decision to lead his army to Rome. During the five years since Cannae, Hannibal had lain awake at night pondering his decision not to attack the walls of Rome when it was weakest. Even though he had won many Italian and overseas allies after Cannae, he must have felt that he had missed his moment. He increasingly found himself trapped in a long, endless war of occupation in a foreign land with no great hope of victory. Seen in this light, his march on Rome could be viewed as Hannibal's final act of recognition that he would never in fact defeat his greatest enemy.

METAURUS

Hannibal's war in Italy was never the greatest concern of the wealthy merchant families of Carthage. They wanted to drive Rome into submission so that they could regain their commercial dominance in the western Mediterranean, but the conquest of the Italian peninsula was simply a means to an end. Even the most fervent supporters of Hannibal simply wanted to beat Rome, turn Italy over to the Italians, and bring the army home. What the Carthaginian aristocracy, who controlled the government and trade, truly cared about was Spain. Many in the ruling classes of Carthage hadn't supported the Barca family when Hannibal's father launched his invasion of Iberia two decades earlier, but they had come to see the vast and wealthy new land as the key to Carthaginian prosperity. Generations before the Barcas had gained control of the mines and riches of Spain, the Carthaginians had forged lasting alliances with the Greek and Phoenician colonies on the Iberian coast, as well as with the many inland tribes. The recent conquest of Spain had not only strengthened those deep ties but made Carthaginian merchants fabulously rich. Defeat the Romans, they all agreed, but when we are done we should leave Italy, for Iberia and its riches are what truly matter. Carthaginian control of Spain must be preserved at all costs.

Carthage's focus on Spain was evident from the beginning of the war. Hannibal's brother Hasdrubal had long planned to follow his brother into Italy with a second army, but native uprisings and Roman threats forced him to remain in Iberia to hold the land for Carthage. Hannibal's other brother Mago had gone to Iberia to recruit troops for Italy after his embassy to Carthage, but again the needs of Spain superseded any problems Hannibal might be facing in Italy. The Carthaginian Senate ordered the two younger Barca brothers to stay in Spain for the time being to secure the country against Rome. The single Barca sibling in Italy would have to make do on his own. The threat to Iberia was especially acute now that the two Scipio brothers, Gnaeus and Publius, were fighting together in Spain with their Roman and allied armies.

In the autumn of 216 B.C.E., just after Hannibal's victory at Cannae, his brother Hasdrubal met the Scipio brothers in battle just south of the Ebro River in northern Spain. But unlike at Cannae, the Carthaginian infantry at the center of the front line collapsed and let the Romans win a huge victory and much of the Carthaginian army present that day was lost. What followed over the next few years was a steady series of Roman victories in Spain, mingled with occasional Carthaginian successes. But at last, the tide turned when Publius Scipio[1] was attacked by a combined force of Carthaginians, Celtiberians, and their new Numidian ally, the young prince Masinissa. Publius died on the battlefield along with most of his legions. This left the remaining Roman forces in Spain under Gnaeus Scipio painfully vulnerable. The Iberians soldiers who had recently joined his Roman army could sense the change in the wind and promptly abandoned their new ally. Hasdrubal and his Carthaginians then chased the Romans north until they had Gnaeus Scipio and his men surrounded on a barren hill. The Roman general fought bravely, as did his men, but in the end he fell beneath the Carthaginian assault along with his soldiers. It seemed as if the war in Spain between the Scipio and the Barca families was at last over with Carthage the clear victor.

When the Roman Senate heard about the fall of the Scipio brothers, almost no one among them wanted to continue the war in Spain. The fight with Hannibal in Italy was going so poorly for Rome that the call to send more troops to Iberia seemed like a waste of badly needed resources. It was at this moment that a young man who had been immersed in the war with Hannibal from the beginning stood up and declared his candidacy for consul with the bold intention of leading the Roman armies in Spain. This was Publius Cornelius Scipio, son of the general of the same name, who had served the Republic so well until he had fallen to the Carthaginians in Spain. The younger Scipio saw it as his sacred duty to continue the war that his father and uncle had waged against the Barca family. The fact that Scipio had never held high office and was legally too young to be elected consul was troublesome to many of the old guard in the senate, but his family name held great weight, not just among the Romans but among the Spanish allies who were accustomed to fighting under a Scipio.

Young Scipio had been shaped by the war with Hannibal like few other Romans. As a teenager he had stood with his father at the Battle of the Ticinus River when the Carthaginians had first crossed the Alps. There he saved the wounded elder Scipio from death and earned a reputation as a resourceful and determined soldier. He had been present as a young military tribune on that terrible day at Cannae, and again loyally fought to save the life of his commander, the not-so-valiant Varro. After the battle, when things seemed darkest for Rome, some of the sons of the Roman elite had considered fleeing Italy to sell their services as mercenary soldiers elsewhere in the Mediterranean. Scipio had rallied his friends and made them swear never to abandon the Republic. Now, at twenty-five years old, he was ready to take up the family mantle and lead in Iberia—the same age as Hannibal had been when he had taken command of the Carthaginian armies in Spain eleven years earlier. The senate was not enthusiastic about young Scipio's chances, but so many Roman magistrates and officers had died in the war with Hannibal that few men were able or willing to lead the armies. Reluctantly they approved the election of Scipio and commissioned him to carry on the war in Spain.

And so, in 210 B.C.E., six years after the Battle of Cannae, young Scipio left Rome and sailed to Spain.[2] He landed with his army at the old Greek colony of Emporium on the northeast coast of the peninsula. From there he moved to Tarraco just north of the Ebro River for the winter. Fearing spies among his allies, he told only his second-in-command Gaius Laelius what he had in mind. The Carthaginians in Spain had grown accustomed to competent, though fairly conventional, fighting from Scipio's slain father and uncle, but the younger man had a much bolder plan—more in the mold of Hannibal himself. Although Scipio had learned a great deal from his family about war, it was the Carthaginian general he had never met who was his true teacher. Like Hannibal, Scipio combined meticulous preparation with swift and unexpected action. The young Roman general spent his first winter in Spain collecting intelligence on his enemy, familiarizing himself with the land, and recruiting allies among any Iberians who had grown disaffected with Carthage. All the while he was planning his daring campaign for the spring.

There were three Carthaginian armies operating in Spain at the time, two under the Barca brothers and one under the commander Hasdrubal Gisgo. The Carthaginians were confident that they had neutralized the Roman threat to Iberia and had little concern about the young commander playing general across the Ebro. They expected a few local skirmishes and posturing by Scipio, but no real threat. The Carthaginians were therefore devoting their resources to fighting rebel Iberian tribes and securing the riches of Spain for their country. The last thing they expected was for Scipio to march his outnumbered army hundreds of miles south of the Ebro and attack their city of New Carthage—but that is exactly what he did.

New Carthage, founded by the Barca family, was the center of Carthaginian power in Spain. It was heavily fortified with massive walls and controlled a key port on the Mediterranean coast. It was also the treasury of the Carthaginians and dominated the lucrative mining operations in the nearby mountains. The Barca brothers had such confidence in the strong fortifications of the town that they had left only a thousand soldiers resident in the city's garrison. The rest of the population were merchants, shopkeepers, and townspeople unprepared for war.

Scipio moved his army across the Ebro and raced down the coast for New Carthage, shadowed by his fleet under his lieutenant Gaius Laelius. Scipio and his army of perhaps twenty-five thousand men were at the walls of city before anyone knew they had left Tarraco. In a coordinated move, his fleet sailed into the harbor of the city at the same time and blockaded the port. The citizens sent word to the Barca brothers, but their armies were at least ten days away. Still, the walls of the city were so formidable that the townspeople were not overly concerned about the arrival of the Romans. The overconfident Carthaginian commander of the city sent his forces out to harass the legions beyond the walls mostly to make a good show for the besieged citizens, but his troops were soon cut down by the Roman army.

Scipio had studied reports about the city and knew from local fishermen that the lagoon beneath the walls, though it looked frightfully deep, was in fact shallow at low tide. When the sea was down, he thus sent his whole army wading across the lagoon with scaling ladders to the city. With the town now virtually unde-fended, the legions were over the walls and in the streets before the citizens knew what was happening. In a single day, the assault on New Carthage and its capture was complete. Scipio, in true Roman fashion, ordered his men to slaughter any man, woman, or child they found, keeping alive only the ones who might fetch a good price on the slave market. The soldiers were allowed to keep whatever valuables they took from their victims or in the houses, but the untold wealth of Carthaginian silver and gold in the city treasury became the property of the senate and people of Rome. Against all odds, the leading Carthaginian city of Spain had quickly fallen to an untried Roman general in his twenties. It was a disaster beyond measure for Carthage and one that would alter the course of the war for Hannibal.

❦

Capua, Syracuse, and now New Carthage—Rome was rap-idly reducing the number of cities Hannibal might rely on for logistical and financial support for his campaign in Italy. The key port of Tarentum[3] in southern Italy was also lost to Fabius Maximus, who had been elected consul again. The unforgiving

Romans slaughtered many of the citizens of the town in revenge for switching sides and sold another thirty thousand into slavery. With the fall of Tarentum, whatever chance Hannibal still had of a military victory in Italy seemed to vanish. He was now further restricted from resupply and reliant on a shrinking alliance of Italians who were still unwilling to yield their freedom to the might of Rome.

In the face of a such despairing odds, why did Hannibal continue to fight? The answer must lie in the fear he continued to inspire among the Romans. Although he was vastly outnumbered and confined to roaming the mountains of southern Italy with his loyal soldiers, he was still a military threat to Rome and an even greater psychological menace. He had beaten the Romans in every major battle in which they were foolish enough to face him. He had killed a large portion of an entire generation of young Roman men. He had exposed the vulnerability of their empire and Italian alliances. He was, in short, the nightmare from which they could not awaken. As long as his army was roaming the countryside of Italy, the Romans could never feel safe.

But the most important reason Hannibal did not take his army and sail back to Carthage was that every year he could force the Romans to commit major military resources to shadowing him in Italy was a year they were not using those troops to make war on his people in Spain or Africa. He also felt a great sense of responsibility to his Italian allies who had chosen to remain with him through the darkest of times. If he abandoned Italy, he knew the Romans would slaughter them, destroy their towns, and sell their families into slavery. Hannibal was also hopeful, and not foolishly so, that his brothers in Spain might yet be able to cross into Italy and reinforce his army for a combined attack on the Romans. If Spain truly became a lost cause, his brothers Hasdrubal[4] and Mago could follow a path over the Alps and press the Romans from the north while he moved against them from the south. The fear of a combined war of the Barca brothers against the Romans in Italy was enough to keep the most confident senators awake at night.

But the Carthaginians were not yet ready to give up on Spain. In the spring of the following year Hasdrubal Barca met the young general Scipio in battle near the town of Baecula in southern Spain. Hasdrubal had almost as much skill in matters of war as his older brother and positioned his army in a favorable spot to face Scipio, who was eager to try his famous luck in facing a Barca brother in open battle. Using unconventional techniques he had learned from Hannibal, Scipio attacked the flanks of Hasdrubal's army and pushed the Carthaginians back. In doing so he caught Hasdrubal's men out of position and was able to drive them back in chaotic retreat, killing at least a third of Hasdrubal's army.

The Battle of Baecula was a devastating blow to the Carthaginians in Spain. They were not yet willing to surrender the country to Rome, but Hasdrubal decided to try to shift the focus of the war back to Italy and relieve pressure on Spain. Hasdrubal led his troops on a roundabout journey west to the Atlantic coast and over the Pyrenees into southern Gaul heading for Italy. Scipio, with uncharacteristic caution, feared this might be a trap and did not follow them. None other than Fabius Maximus in Rome criticized the young general for excess timidity.

Back in Italy, Hannibal was thrilled with the news that his brother was on the way with a large Carthaginian army. But the Romans were now determined anew to crush Hannibal in Italy before he could link up with his brother. Since Hannibal had fewer men than in the past and had been increasingly restricted in the size of his operating territory, Rome felt it might finally be able to deliver the fatal blow. The two consuls for the year were Marcus

Claudius Marcellus, the veteran conqueror of Syracuse, and Titus Quinctius Crispinus, also no stranger to war. They moved their armies south and coordinated their efforts to provoke Hannibal into battle. Each day they would boldly lead their armies out of camp and approach Hannibal's smaller army, daring him to fight. One day, the consuls rode out to survey a hill near the Roman camp to survey with a small force in hope of using it to surprise Hannibal. But the Carthaginian commander was as usual one step ahead of the Romans. He had already hidden a troop of his Numidian cavalry behind the hill, which attacked the consuls from the rear. Crispinus was injured by javelins and fled, while Marcellus was run through with a sword in close combat. Both consuls, proven generals that they were, had foolishly fallen into a classic trap. Hannibal ordered the body of his foe Marcellus properly adorned and cremated with honor.

Hannibal, as well as all of Rome, waited for Hasdrubal to emerge from Gaul into Italy. Over a decade earlier, Hannibal had led an army in early winter over the Alps with huge losses, but Hasdrubal was not constrained by threatening Roman armies and so chose a lower and much faster route across the mountains. By summer he was in the Po River valley recruiting a new generation of Celtic warriors and harassing Roman settlements along the way. By the time he left northern Italy, his army may have numbered thirty-five thousand troops along with a number of battle elephants. When Hannibal heard the good news, he prepared to lead his army north to rendezvous with his brother. The Carthaginian hope of victory in Italy was alive once again.

The city of Rome was thrown into yet another panic by the approach of not one, but two, Barca brothers. The new consuls for the year, Gaius Claudius Nero and Marcus Livius Salinator, divided their forces and each headed toward a different Carthaginian army. They were desperate to keep the two enemy generals apart since a united Carthaginian force might well be able to undo all the victories they had gained since Cannae. This was made much easier when the Romans captured Carthaginian messengers from Hasdrubal to his brother with letters detailing their plan of attack. The brothers were planning to meet in Umbria, so before this could happen, the consuls quickly rejoined forces and focused their efforts on Hasdrubal alone, betting they could defeat the northern Carthaginian army before Hannibal could reach them.

Soon Hasdrubal realized he was facing two Roman consuls and an army that outnumbered his own. Knowing that the key to victory was to combine his own forces with his brother's, Hasdrubal avoided battle and retreated by night until he came to the Metaurus River in the central Italian hills. As he was attempting to lead his army across, the Romans attacked. Hasdrubal was caught off guard in unfamiliar country and forced into battle unprepared. Though a fine general and brave warrior, fate and circumstances united against him that fateful day. The Romans were able to outflank him using techniques they had learned from Hannibal, destroying the Carthaginian army. Hasdrubal, fighting beside his men until the end, fell beneath a Roman sword. When the news reached Rome, the senate declared three days of public celebrations. Instead of allowing their foe a proper burial, the Romans cut off Hasdrubal's head and had it thrown over the walls of Hannibal's camp. According to Livy, in his brother's death and mutilation, Hannibal saw the looming destiny of Carthage.

~~~

H asdrubal was dead, but Hannibal's brother Mago was still waging war in Spain against Scipio and his Roman armies.

Along with his fellow general Hasdrubal Gisgo, Mago had raised an enormous army of at least fifty thousand soldiers from the Iberian natives still loyal to Carthage. In the early spring of 206 B.C.E., just north of modern Seville, the Carthaginians and Romans met near the town of Ilipa.⁵ Scipio was outnumbered by several thousand men, but he had learned war from Hannibal, the best of teachers. At the Battle of Trebia in northern Italy twelve years earlier, Hannibal had made sure his men were well-fed and rested before a surprise attack on the Romans. Now in distant Spain, Scipio did the same. The Carthaginian army was caught totally off guard in an early morning assault and confronted by a series of tactical battle maneuvers that Hannibal himself would have been proud of. The Carthaginian survivors retreated and Hasdrubal Gisgo fled to Gades, from which he sailed back to Africa. Mago remained in Gades for a time with the remnants of the Carthaginian army until he also was ordered to abandon Iberia with the Carthaginian fleet and army. After a futile attempt to retake New Carthage by sea, Mago sailed on to Liguria in northern Italy where he captured the port city of Genoa. The younger Barca brother was able to hold the town and use it as a base for local raids for two years, but he was little more than an annoyance to the Romans.

Scipio spent the rest of the year crushing any resistance that remained in Spain. Among the towns punished for their loyalty to Carthage were Illurgia and Astapa. At Illurgia he directed his troops to take no prisoners, even massacring infants ripped from their mothers' arms. When the townspeople of Astapa heard the news, they chose mass suicide over surrender. The Romans showed no mercy to the Iberians as they consolidated their control of the peninsula and secured its riches for themselves.

Hannibal spent the next few years based in Bruttium in the toe of Italy. He was still a threat and certainly a force the Romans could not ignore, but even the most ardent of his Carthaginian supporters now realized that it was just a matter of time until he was killed or withdrew to Africa. Hannibal knew however that every year he could maintain his army in Italy was time he could divert Roman resources away from an attack on Africa. He was also still most reluctant to abandon the Italians who had served him so well during the dozen years he had waged war against the Romans in their homeland. He worked tirelessly to protect his allies and care for his soldiers, many of whom had grown old with him since they had crossed the Alps together as young men. Scarred by countless battles and graying though they might be, their devotion to their commander was absolute and speaks volumes about the kind of man that Hannibal was.

ZAMA

The noose was slowly tightening on Carthage. Spain and Sicily had fallen to the Romans, Hannibal was restricted to an ever-shrinking region in the toe of Italy, and now some of the Numidians—stalwart allies of Carthage and the source of their matchless cavalry—were beginning to wonder if they had chosen the wrong side in the war with Rome. Aside from being so important to the Carthaginian military, the Numidians occupied the vast lands to the west of the city along the northern African coast all the way to the Atlantic Ocean. If they could be persuaded to join the Romans, Carthage would lose the strongest force in their army and be open to invasion from the west. The young Numidian prince Masinissa knew the situation better than most and secretly opened negotiations with Scipio after the Battle of Ilipa to see what advantages he might gain by abandoning his Carthaginian allies. Masinissa was, however, a king without a kingdom. His late father's territory in Africa was ruled by a distant relative, while the western regions of Numidia were governed by the wily old king Syphax, a ruler who enjoyed playing the Romans and Carthaginians off against each other to his own advantage. Masinissa's only assets were his name and matchless ambition. For Scipio, this was enough to welcome the young man as a new friend of the senate and people of Rome.

After winning Masinissa to his side, Scipio returned from Spain to Rome for the consular elections of 205 B.C.E.. He had impressed the city not only with his Iberian victories but by the shiploads of treasure and slaves he brought back for the Roman people. Many of the old guard in the senate still viewed him suspiciously as an upstart boy, but he charmed the common people and easily won another term as consul. Chief among his campaign themes was the need to take the war directly to Africa to finish it. Some senators, including Fabius Maximus, objected that Hannibal was still a grave threat in Italy and must be dealt with before any invasion of the Carthaginian homeland. But the younger generation of senate leaders sided with Scipio and eventually prevailed. Rome had grown wealthy on aggressive conquest. If they could defeat Carthage in Africa, there would be no limit to their ambitions—and profits—in the Mediterranean and beyond.

After Scipio arrived in Sicily and set up headquarters, he carefully prepared for the invasion of Africa in the coming year. In the meantime, he sent his trusted lieutenant Laelius to raid the coast around Carthage and stir up fear among its people. The Carthaginians knew an invasion was inevitable, so they did everything possible to blunt its impact. Orders were sent to Hannibal and Mago in Italy to delay as many legions as possible there, though the options for both brothers to do so were limited. Carthage also began a renewed effort to win the Numidian king Syphax firmly to their side. The ruler was known to have an eye for beautiful women, so the Carthaginians offered him a bride named Sophonisba, the daughter of the general Hasdrubal Gisgo. This was exactly what was needed. Syphax sent Scipio a message saying that because of his new marriage, he would reluctantly be obligated to fight on the Carthaginian side in the case of a Roman invasion.

The young prince Masinissa[1] meanwhile was struggling to regain his father's kingdom. He crossed over from Spain and started to rally allies along the western coast of Mediterranean Africa. But Syphax was still a powerful force in the region and soon countered Masinissa, defeating him in battle and forcing him to take refuge in the mountains. Syphax tracked him there and bested him again so that the prince fled into the wilderness with only a few dozen men. It seemed as if Masinissa would no longer be a threat to Carthage in the war.

If the Romans were counting out Hannibal while they were preparing to invade Africa, they soon learned that the Carthaginian general was yet a force to be reckoned with. Hannibal still controlled the major port of Locri[2] in the toe of Italy, a town with not one, but two, major defensive citadels within its walls. His allies in the city had remained loyal to him for many years, but some of the local merchants were growing weary of the economic losses they were suffering in the midst of the endless war. They approached Scipio and offered to betray their town to the Romans in exchange for favorable terms for themselves. Scipio jumped at the opportunity and sent troops from Sicily to the port by night and seized one of the two citadels for the Romans. The Carthaginians still held the other, with the unfortunates residents of Locri now trapped between two hostile armies. Hannibal soon arrived at the walls of the city with a small relief force and attacked the part controlled by the Romans. At the same time, Scipio himself sailed into Locri with a large number of troops. The outnumbered Hannibal was now faced with the choice of abandoning a faithful ally or confronting Scipio in what he knew would be a losing battle of urban warfare. Reluctantly he withdrew his soldiers back into the mountains to fight another day, saving them for the greater battle in Africa that he knew was coming. Scipio and the vengeful Romans massacred the inhabitants of Locri and committed atrocities even later Roman writers were ashamed to admit.

∽

In the spring of 204 B.C.E., Scipio and his Roman army left Sicily and landed at last on the coast of Africa. They established their camp near the Carthaginian town of Utica, not far to the north of the capital city. Panic spread throughout the land and Carthage itself suffered the same terror that had swept Rome years before when Hannibal arrived at their city gates. The elders of the city knew they were outnumbered and had no general at hand who could defeat Scipio and his forces. But they were not going to give up easily. While Scipio was besieging Utica, they sent Hasdrubal Gisgo and King Syphax to attack him with a combined force of perhaps fifty thousand men. Outnumbered, Scipio withdrew from Utica and set up a fortified winter camp near the Bagradas River north of Carthage, while the Africans pitched their own camp nearby to keep a careful eye on him. His ambitious invasion of Africa had ground to a sudden halt.

But any Carthaginian who dismissed the Scipio's considerable cleverness was foolish indeed. He began negotiations with Carthage through Syphax to discuss a possible end to the war, based on Hannibal's withdrawal from Italy and his own from Africa. This was, however, merely a ruse to lure the Carthaginians into lowering their guard. In his reconnoitering of the countryside, Scipio had noticed that the Carthaginian winter camp was built almost entirely of wood, with troop huts made of reeds and thatch. This was a mistake Hannibal never would have made, which Scipio was quick to take advantage of. He created a diversion by leading his army suddenly towards Utica while he sent his lieutenant Laelius to the Carthaginian camp with torches. At just the right moment in the night, they threw the firebrands over the walls and set a raging inferno ablaze in the camp. Livy says that forty thousand men were burned alive[3] or cut down as they fled the fires, which is surely an exaggeration, but the casualties must have numbered in the many of thousands. Hasdrubal Gisgo and Syphax escaped, however, and soon recruited more men, though many of them must have been poorly equipped local farmers pressed into service. Bravely but foolishly they marched on Scipio as he was besieging Utica and met him in open battle at a place called the Great Plains. The Romans easily defeated this makeshift army and gained a huge advantage in the war. Carthage had few troops left to fight the Romans and could do little more than hide behind their massive walls as Scipio and his men raged throughout the countryside.

Syphax had fled back to his kingdom after the losing battle, pursued by a resurgent Masinissa. He caught up with the old king near his stronghold of Cirta, where Masinissa captured and paraded Syphax in chains through the streets. The young prince also took Syphax's wife Sophonisba[4] as prisoner and was contemplating what to do with her when she threw herself at his feet and begged him not to hand her over to the Romans. Masinissa was moved by her pleas and beauty, and so decided that there could be no sweeter revenge on old Syphax than to take his young wife for his own bride. As a captive in war, such a marriage to a defeated queen was traditional and expected by his Numidian supporters. Scipio however was livid at the news since he had planned to parade Sophonisba through Rome as centerpiece of his triumphal parade. He insisted that the woman be surrendered to him at once. Masinissa was now in the unenviable position of disobeying Scipio and losing Roman support for his rule or handing over his bride and losing all respect from his African followers. As a third option, he gave Sophonisba a cup of poison to drink, which she freely downed, denying Scipio his prize.

The people of Carthage now realized they were in an impossible situation. They didn't have enough soldiers to push the Romans out of Africa or even face them on the battlefield. Hannibal and his army were far away in Italy and would take months at top speed to reach Carthage. Businessmen that they were, the elders of Carthage decided to make a deal with the Romans. A group of thirty leading citizens made their way to Scipio's headquarters to negotiate a peace treaty. Coming to the general they bowed to the ground before him and immediately placed all of the blame for the war on Hannibal. Scipio knew this was a lie, but he also realized he was not in a position to take the well-fortified city of Carthage. He was also a reasonable man who had no great desire to destroy the enemy city completely. Better to thoroughly humble it and expand the power as well as status of Rome. His peace terms were therefore harsh but not exceedingly so given the current situation between the two nations. The Carthaginians would have to evacuate their troops from Italy and anywhere else beyond Africa. They were to return all Roman prisoners unharmed, along with any deserters from the legions to suffer crucifixion. They were to surrender their entire navy aside from twenty warships, which could only patrol the African coast. Finally, they were to provide the Romans with grain from their fields and storehouses, as well as pay a huge indemnity in cash, much as they had done at the end of the previous war. Since they had few real options, the Carthaginian elders agreed to all of Scipio's terms. They then sent a delegation of the leaders of the Carthaginian government to Rome to ratify the treaty before the senate. Livy, always hostile to Carthage, claims that Carthage was never serious about negotiating and only wanted to buy time to renew the war. He even says that the treaty wasn't ratified by Rome. This is unlikely and contradicts Polybius, who is usually more reliable when the two historians disagree. According to the latter, the negotiations were successfully concluded and the treaty ratified by both Rome and Carthage.

When the peace talks were concluded, Carthage sent messengers to Hannibal in Italy with the orders he had long been expecting—he was to evacuate Italy and return to Africa. Similar orders were sent to Hannibal's brother Mago in Genoa, but the younger sibling died from battle wounds en route to Africa. Now only one Barca brother remained alive. Hannibal would be forced to leave behind the Italians who had served him so faithfully, many from the earliest days of the war. He would be able to transport some of his troops back to Africa, but the townspeople of southern Italy who had sided with him had to be left behind. Neither they nor Hannibal had any illusions about what the Romans would do to them in their revenge.

∞

Thus in the year 203 B.C.E., fifteen years after first arriving in Italy, Hannibal watched from his ship as the mountains of southern Italy passed beyond the horizon. He had left Carthage for Spain when he was only a boy and had marched into Italy as a young man. Now he was in his midforties, going home to a place he barely remembered. It was also a city that had turned against him, blaming him for all the suffering they were experiencing while conveniently forgetting about all he had done for his country. Certain he would receive no warm welcome and perhaps even be imprisoned at Carthage, he turned the ships southward and landed at last in Africa near his family estates in the rich farmlands around Hadrumetum far from the city. This was the place of his boyhood memories and a safe base from which to watch and see what happened next between Carthage and Rome. He, for one, had little faith that the Romans would abide by the terms of the treaty.

Scipio remained in Africa with his army to keep a watchful eye on Carthage. The Carthaginians had agreed to keep his army supplied with food even though they were short on supplies themselves and growing more hungry each day. The requisitioning of Carthaginian food for the legions seems more of a deliberate humiliation and punishment than a necessity as the Roman troops in Africa were receiving steady shipments of grain from Rome throughout the winter. When one of these Roman freight convoys was caught in a storm and blown away from Scipio's camp, it washed up near the city of Carthage. The townspeople on the walls could see the floundered ships in the distance and called a meeting of their senate to decide what to do. They were desperate for food and most considered the wrecked Roman ships fair game for a salvage operation. Others thought it would only provoke a violent reaction from Scipio. In the end, hunger won the debate and the Carthaginians towed the transports back to the city, helping themselves to the grain onboard.

When Scipio heard what the Carthaginians had done he was angry, not so much about the food, which he wouldn't miss, but because of the threat to his fragile peace. He was also afraid that the seizure of the convoy would damage his reputation among his opposition in Rome. Many senators were increasingly jealous of his success, first in Spain and now in Africa. Any opportunity to remove him from command would be eagerly seized upon by the conservatives in Rome. Scipio's only option, as much as he might not like it, was to strike back hard against Carthage and punish them severely. He first sent envoys to the Carthaginian Senate and demanded they hand over the grain, though he knew it had surely already been distributed to the hungry people. The Carthaginians were tired of Roman demands by now and sent the envoys away, with some hotheads among them actually attacking their ship as they returned to the Roman camp. This gave Scipio all the excuse he needed. He began to assault Carthaginian cities up and down the coast, killing many of the inhabitants and selling the rest into slavery. He knew this would mean an end to the negotiated peace between Rome and Carthage, but events were now beyond his control. He also hoped the attacks might provoke Hannibal out of his hiding place at his estates far south of Carthage. His respect for his adversary was genuine, but he believed a final, glorious victory against the legendary Carthaginian general would seal his reputation for all time.

The Carthaginians had already sent messengers to Hannibal begging him to defend his native city. Just a short time earlier they had turned on their most famous son and blamed him for the dire situation in which they now found themselves, but they were not above seeking his help in the current disaster. Hannibal was not inclined to rush to the city's defense since the wealthy merchants who governed Carthage had been strictly fair-weather friends to the Barca family. But he was in his heart a son of Carthage and felt a deep connection and responsibility to the common people there who had supported him and his family over the years. Even though he knew the odds were greatly against him, Hannibal could not abandon his people when they called on him. His most pressing problem was that he had been forced to leave most of his horses behind in Italy. The timely arrival of two thousand rebel Numidian cavalry at Hannibal's headquarters gave him hope that he might be able to teach Rome one final lesson. And so, Hannibal gathered his forces and marched west a few days inland near Scipio's camp at a place called Zama.

Never one to leave anything to chance, Hannibal sent out three trusted scouts to spy on Scipio's position and report back to him. These men were captured by an alert Roman patrol and brought before Scipio. Instead of torturing them to death as was standard Roman practice, the Roman general personally showed them around his camp and sent them safely back to Hannibal to relate what they had seen. It was a smart move on the confident Scipio's part to prove to Hannibal he was not at all afraid of his famous enemy. It might have worked on a lesser general, but Hannibal had practically written the manual of the psychology of war. The Carthaginian commander sent Scipio a note thanking him for showing such kindness to his men and inviting him to a one-on-one meeting so the two of them could talk in person.[5]

This was not what Scipio was expecting, but rather than show any fear, he agreed to the meeting. Hannibal then moved his camp even closer to the Roman position, perhaps to further discomfort Scipio. Both sides were now busy preparing themselves for the final battle. But the day before it would take place, Hannibal and Scipio, each with a small escort, rode out of their camps to a quiet place between the two armies. Leaving even these men behind, the two greatest generals of the age then dismounted and met in the middle, just the two of them. Some ancient sources say they used translators, but this is unlikely. The conversation between the men was probably spoken in Greek, which both knew well. Hannibal greeted Scipio first and thanked him for agreeing to the meeting. He felt no anger against the Roman commander with whom he had more in common than perhaps anyone else on earth. Both men were brilliant strategists and tacticians of war who had long admired the accomplishments of the other. Both were also men with a deep love for their respective countries in spite of how badly their own people might have treated them. Hannibal spoke of the endless and bloody war he had led in Italy and sought a way to end the conflict without any more deaths. Scipio shook his head and said it was, sadly, too late for that. Events had overtaken them both and political pressures at home would not allow him to walk away. Only a final battle could bring the war to an end. The generals then rode back to their camps to ready their armies for the next day.

Thus, one morning in the autumn of 202 B.C.E., the Carthaginian and Romans armies met for the final time on the plain of Zama.[6] Hannibal was driven by duty to defend his city, though he had little hope that he could beat Scipio and the hardened legions of Rome in open battle. His army that day was a shadow of what it had been at Trasimene or Cannae. Several thousand mercenaries who had served his brother Mago at Genoa had arrived for the fight, but they fought solely for money and had little enthusiasm for the battle ahead. Numidian refugees and Carthaginian volunteers with little experience with fighting made up much of the rest of the army. Only a small core group of troops who had fought with Hannibal in Italy were present that day. These he kept close to himself as he lined up his troops. What he most painfully lacked as he faced Scipio was cavalry. With only a few thousand horsemen at his command on the open plains of Zama, he was at a huge disadvantage to the Romans. Still, Hannibal was determined to make the best stand he could in what he knew would be his final effort to save his country.

Scipio lined up his legions with great gaps in his formation—a technique he knew would be effective in allowing the Carthaginian elephants to pass through his lines without causing much damage. Indeed, when the battle began the elephants panicked and charged back against their own lines, throwing Hannibal's lines into chaos. That was just the start of a disastrous day for Carthage. The mercenaries at the front of Hannibal's troops pushed the Romans back at first, but then retreated under heavy fire and attacked the Carthaginian forces behind them to escape. The battle quickly devolved into bloody slaughter. Scipio was able to cut easily through the Carthaginian lines and kill many thousands of enemy soldiers. Hannibal and his core of veterans fought bravely and for long as they could, but when it was clear that the Romans had won the day, he retreated to his estates at Hadrumentum with his few surviving men. The war between Carthage and Rome, fought so long and well by Hannibal until the very end, was now truly over.

EXILE

Carthage had a long record of executing failed generals, even when they had done their best against impossible odds. Hannibal had good reason to expect his native city would do the same to him, especially as they already blamed him for the loss of the war. It was therefore a remarkable act of patriotism that when Hannibal was summoned to the Carthaginian Senate from his estates after the defeat at Zama, he answered the call and went back to the city.

Hannibal was now in his midforties. He had left Carthage at the age of nine and not been back since. The city had grown rich through the gold and silver of Spain that had poured into the town over the last few decades, thanks to the Barca family. As Hannibal rode through the familiar lanes on the way to the senate house, he saw fine new homes of rich merchants on the Byrsa Hill and elaborate temples filled with treasure. The common people had also greatly benefited from all that his family had done for the city. Everyone watched in wonder as Hannibal himself, more of a legend than a man, rode through the streets up to the senate house. There he dismounted and went inside to address the elders and leaders of the city. Some in the chamber despised him for starting the war, others for not destroying Rome after the victory at Cannae. There were even some who still wanted to fight Rome and hoped that Hannibal might yet lead them to victory. But he shook his head and said no. The war was over and lost. This was the time to make peace with the Romans, now and forever.

Rome's new terms for peace[1] were even harsher than those dictated before Zama. In addition to all previous provisions Scipio had negotiated, Carthage would now have to pay an astonishing ten thousand talents to Rome over the next fifty years. Typically, the wealthy senators of Carthage insisted that the money come from a new tax on the struggling famers rather than paying it themselves. The Carthaginians would also surrender one hundred of their young men, personally chosen by Scipio, from the leading families of the city to serve as hostages in Rome as a guarantee of the city's good behavior. If Carthage rebelled or even looked like it might stray from the treaty, the young hostages would be tortured to death. The city would also have to turn over all its war elephants to Rome and watch from the walls as their war fleet was burned in the harbor. Carthage was forbidden from having any political dealings with nations outside of Africa and they would have to seek Rome's permission before engaging in any war, defensive though it might be. Nearby to the west, Masinissa was allowed to take large amounts of Carthaginian territory along the North African coast for his Numidian kingdom. He was now an important Roman ally and would be tasked with keeping a close eye on Carthage.

Hannibal supported all these measures to save his city. Surprisingly, the Romans did not demand his own surrender. At the end of any other conflict, a defeated enemy leader would have been marched through the streets of Rome in shame as a trophy before being publicly executed. One can see the hand of Scipio in the kinder treatment of Hannibal. Though the Carthaginian general was his most bitter rival in war, in peace he was a defeated opponent who deserved respect. Nor did Scipio allow the Carthaginians to touch Hannibal. There is evidence from later sources that the city did put Hannibal on trial for failing to capture Rome and for greedily keeping the plunder of Italy for himself. Given that he needed whatever he could take in Italy to keep his army going, the latter charge was absurd. But in any case, he was acquitted of all crimes, with Scipio's influence certainly on the mind of the jurors. And so at last when the final treaty was signed and ratified, Hannibal left Carthage and returned to his country estates far south of the city to live a quiet life for the next few years.

The Roman historians we rely on for Hannibal's life story lose interest in the retired general after the war. Rome moved on to other wars and conquests, notably against the Hellenistic kingdom of Seleucid King Antiochus III in the eastern Mediterranean. We hear nothing of Hannibal until six years later when he appears back in Carthage after being elected as one of the two *suffetes*,[2] or chief executive officers, of the city for the coming year. Why Hannibal chose to leave his estates to plunge into the bruising politics of Carthage is a mystery, but simple concern for his city seems a likely reason. Hannibal's hometown had been devastated by the war with Rome and badly needed a steady hand to rebuild itself and take care of its people. From what little we know, Hannibal threw himself into his work with the same energy and administrative skill he had honed over years of leading an army. He organized the state finances so that Carthage could pay its war reparations to Rome without starving the common people. He supervised projects that helped the merchant fleet again trade up and down the African coast. Hannibal was so successful in building up Carthage's new merchant connections that the city would in fact offer to pay back the entire war indemnity to Rome forty years early. But he also raised the ire of the greedy Carthaginian elite by attempting to transfer some of their coveted power to the common people. This was enough to unite the aristocracy firmly against Hannibal in spite of the renewed prosperity Hannibal had helped them achieve. They began to whisper among themselves that their famous general had to be removed from the city's political life forever and so sent misleading letters to the Roman Senate that Rome's greatest enemy was becoming a new threat to Italy by conspiring with Antiochus.

The conservatives in Roman government had never accepted that Hannibal had been allowed to walk free after the war. They were willing to believe, evidence or not, that he was in league with Antiochus to overthrow Rome. Scipio himself spoke up for Hannibal in the senate, but his influence was fading and he was unable to change the mind of the old guard. The senate sent orders to Carthage to arrest and condemn Hannibal for plotting war with Antiochus. The Carthaginian leaders were all too happy to comply and immediately declared him an outlaw and enemy of the state. Hannibal was wisely out of the city at the time, so his opponents vented their anger by burning down the small home he kept in Carthage.

Hannibal now faced an impossible situation. He could retreat to his estates in the south, but he knew the Carthaginians and Romans would never allow him to remain there in peace. He was too important a symbol to be allowed to slip back into obscurity. His only option was to flee Africa and live out his life beyond the grasp of Rome, if such a thing was still possible. So, before his enemies could find him, he said goodbye to his boyhood home and sailed to the nearby island of Kerkennah where merchants gathered from many lands. There he found a Phoenician trading vessel heading for the city of Tyre on the distant coast of Lebanon. Hannibal's ancestors had left Tyre centuries before to found Carthage, so it seemed fitting that he return to the ancient home of his people. Tyre was also at this time part of the Seleucid kingdom of Antiochus, with whom Hannibal had been accused of conspiring. His choice for a place of exile would only have confirmed what his enemies said about him. As unlikely as it was that Hannibal had previously worked secretly with Antiochus against Rome, now he decided he had little to lose by doing so. The opposition in Carthage and Rome would never allow him to return home and would undoubtably hound him across the earth until he was dead or captured. Although he had advocated for peace with Rome at the end of the war, the Romans had now pushed him again into being their enemy. If his own country would not support him, he would serve any ruler in the Mediterranean who was still willing to stand up to Rome.

Hannibal made his way from Tyre to Ephesus on the Aegean coast of Asia Minor where Antiochus was holding court. There he met the king for the first time and offered his services against Rome. Antiochus welcomed Hannibal but did not completely trust him. Many of his advisors counseled him that Hannibal was too much of a target for Roman anger and would push them into war before they were ready. Hannibal, now in his fifties, was thereafter neither completely in nor out of Antiochus's service. He was an exile always on the fringes of the court, waiting, hoping to be useful. It was a new and most uncomfortable position for a man who had spent his life in action. With little to do, one day he reportedly attended a lecture in Ephesus by a renowned philosopher named Phormio who fancied himself an expert on military affairs. After listening to the teacher lecture on the qualities of an ideal general, Hannibal stood up and told him frankly, in Greek, that he didn't have the faintest idea what he was talking about. Even in his later years, Hannibal never minced words nor did he suffer fools gladly.

Ephesus was also reportedly the scene for a meeting between Hannibal and his old rival Scipio. The Roman general—now bearing the title Africanus for his victory over the Carthaginians—had been sent by the senate as an envoy to Antiochus. Scipio was now a middle-aged man out of favor in Rome. The two former enemies greeted each other warmly and spoke of old battles and the vagaries of fortune. After several glasses of wine, Scipio asked Hannibal who he considered the greatest general in history. Alexander was his reply, to which Scipio heartily agreed. He then asked Hannibal who he considered second best, to which the Carthaginian replied Pyrrhus, who had boldly invaded Italy a century earlier and caused the Romans such trouble before his ultimate defeat. Scipio again concurred. But now the Roman asked who was the third greatest, thinking that he would confer the honor on him as victor over the unbeatable Hannibal. But the Carthaginian only smiled and said he humbly believed that he himself had earned that title, since he had marched an army across the Alps and struck terror into Rome for years with little help from Carthage before his final defeat. Scipio laughed and asked where he would have placed himself on the list if he had been able to conquer Rome. Hannibal confessed that he would then have stood before Alexander.

This was the last time Scipio and his old rival would meet. After this, Hannibal remained in the service of Antiochus, but was given little to do. Later stories claim he was secretly recruiting agents in

Africa to urge Carthage to rise up against Rome, but this seems unlikely. Hannibal was a man of action, not intrigue. There are reports that he may have gotten his wish when, at the age of fifty-seven, he was given command of a few ships as Antiochus faced the Romans in a great naval battle at Magnesia. The Seleucid king was defeated, however, and Hannibal was forced to flee Antiochus's court permanently. Stories of Hannibal are few after that, but the picture we do have is of an aging warrior in his sixties traveling between kingdoms trying to warn those few independent nations still left in the Mediterranean that Rome was coming for them. He may have sailed to the island of Crete, then on to Armenia, before finally traveling to Bithynia in northwest Asia Minor to the court of King Prusias, who was at war with the nearby Attalid king Eumenes, a Roman ally. In a tale that seems imaginative but could possibly be true, Hannibal reportedly commanded Prusias's small Bithynian fleet against Eumenes in a naval battle and defeated him by launching poisonous snakes onto his ships. This could be pure fiction, but it was the sort of unconventional tactic a younger Hannibal might have tried against the Romans.

When Prusias nonetheless lost the war, one of the terms of surrender was that Hannibal be handed over to the Romans. So powerful was the terror that Hannibal evoked in Roman minds that even many years after his defeat, they were still hunting the aging general across the seas. Hannibal was by then a frail old man living in retirement in the small town of Libyssa in Asia Minor. Even though he posed no threat to Rome, the senate and people of Rome would not let him rest. They still wanted to parade the tired old soldier through the streets of their city in triumph. Some stories say that when the detachment of Roman soldiers arrived at his house to seize him, he swallowed the pill of poison that he always carried with him concealed in a ring on his finger. Others report he drank a poisoned cup of wine and confessed with his last breath that he pitied the Romans who could not wait for the natural death of a sick old man. Whatever the details, Hannibal, in his final act of defiance, would not allow his greatest enemy to take him alive. He would not be a prize for the vulgar amusement of the crowd in the Forum. He died alone far from his beloved Carthage, on his own terms, in a last, quiet battle against Rome.

LEGACY

Hannibal was not alone in dying far from home, scorned by a city for which he had done so much. Scipio was also hounded to the end by adversaries jealous of his success and determined to destroy both his career and legacy. The conservative faction of the Roman Senate, led by Marcus Porcius Cato, brought charges against him after his trip to the court of King Antiochus and claimed, without evidence, that he had accepted bribes from the Hellenistic ruler to betray Rome. Anyone who knew Scipio realized this was absurd, but rumor and scandal easily take on a life of their own. Scipio was a master of battlefield tactics, but he had no patience for the petty, backstabbing politics of the senate. He was acquitted of the charges but chose to leave Rome behind forever even though he was only in his fifties and should have enjoyed many more years as a respected elder statesman. He retired to his country estates at Liternum in Campania and never returned to Rome. Bitter and heartbroken at the betrayal of his city, he died in the same year as Hannibal. The world is seldom kind to great men. He instructed his family to bury him in Campania, far from Rome. Two centuries later, a more appreciative Roman, Valerius Maximus,[1] records that Scipio composed his own epitaph: "Ungrateful fatherland, you will not even have my bones."

The same Cato who had driven Scipio from Rome was determined that he would bring an end to Hannibal's city. He had visited Carthage after Hannibal had helped to revitalize the town and was stunned by how the greatest foe of Rome had recovered and prospered. Carthage now posed what Cato considered to again be a grave threat to Roman power. When he returned to the senate, every speech he gave on any subject always ended with the phrase: *Carthago delenda est*—"Carthage must be destroyed!" Eventually in 149 B.C.E., thirty-five years after the death of Hannibal, he persuaded the city elders to launch a third and final war against Carthage. The conflict was led by another Scipio, Aemilianus, the adopted grandson of Scipio Africanus. But if the Romans thought it would be an easy conquest, they were soon proven wrong. The Carthaginians fought ferociously against Rome for four years before their walls were finally broken down and the city taken after days of vicious street-by-street urban combat. The Carthaginians who somehow survived were sold into slavery and the city itself was razed to the ground. To render the site uninhabitable for all time, Roman priests uttered ancient curses over the ruins. The profound spirit of fear that Carthage had evoked in Rome was at last laid to rest.

But as they would one day realize, the Romans owed a debt to Hannibal for what they became. One could reasonably argue that without the greatest enemy they had ever faced, Rome never would have spread across the Mediterranean and established a civilization that, for better or worse, changed the world. The Romans were skilled and ambitious soldiers before their conflict with Carthage, but it was Hannibal who molded them in the crucible of war. From Hannibal, the Romans first learned to fight beyond Italy in long-term conflicts that demanded a professional military far beyond their traditional army of farmers led by amateur generals. He forced them to adapt their fighting techniques to overcome unfamiliar tactics and superior strategies. He pushed them to look beyond Italy and provoked them into invading Spain, the first major overseas province in the Roman empire. In time, Rome may have expanded far beyond Italy without Hannibal's influence, but he and the threat he embodied were the prime catalysts for their ultimate imperial expansion from Spain and Britain to Syria and Egypt. Hannibal was the best teacher of war that Rome ever had. He also became a terror that lived in their nightmares. In centuries to come, whenever they debated whether a foreign people were a threat to their country, they remembered Hannibal marching over the Alps. In an effort never to permit such a thing to happen again, they became one of the most aggressive imperial powers in the history of the world. Hannibal may have taken his own life in a distant land, but his ghost haunted the streets of Rome for generations.

Almost four hundred years after Hannibal died, a new dynasty of Roman emperors, the Severans, came to power and prompted Rome to look at the African general in a new way. By then the Roman Empire had long encompassed and embraced many foreign cultures. Ambitious and talented leaders need not have been born to the ancient nobility of the city of Rome itself, but could be from anywhere in the empire. Septimius Severus, the first of the Severan dynasty, was an African from Libya who traced his roots back to the same Punic settlers who had built Carthage. Septimius saw Hannibal as a distant member of his own family and began the rehabilitation of his reputation. He rebuilt the worn tomb of Hannibal in Bithynia so that it became a place of pilgrimage for Romans and others from all over the Mediterranean. Many wanted to see the grave of the man who had almost destroyed Rome and yet ultimately helped created the empire it had become.

Stories of Hannibal were told for many years after Rome itself fell. Medieval Europe largely knew of him from the pages of Livy, the most hostile historian to the African leader. And yet Hannibal was a man much admired in the Middle Ages for his daring, honor, and matchless military skill. Generals from all ages studied and continue to study Hannibal's techniques of facing a superior enemy in battle and turning disadvantage to victory. Napoleon was perhaps the greatest admirer of Hannibal, but countless students of history have followed in their imaginations as he led his battle elephants through the Alps and crushed the Romans at Trasimene and Cannae.

In the end, how we view Hannibal depends on what we want to see in the man. No one today easily looks at a leader who slaughtered tens of thousands on the battlefield as a noble hero or model for emulation. We thankfully live in a different age from Alexander the Great, Julius Caesar, or Hannibal. But if we are able to judge a person by the standards of their own violent time, Hannibal does not fare badly in his potential for clemency or willingness to fight what he considered a just war against an enemy determined to annihilate his country and people. Even the Romans, in their fear and hatred of Hannibal, could not help but admire his determination, brilliance, and ultimately his humanity. We should do nothing less.

EPILOGUE

WHAT IF HANNIBAL HAD WON?

If it is true—which no one doubts—that the Romans surpass all nations in strength, it must not be denied that Hannibal surpassed other commanders in ability by as much as the Roman people exceed all nations in determination. For whenever he met the Romans in battle in Italy, he always won. If he had not been held back by the jealousy of his own citizens at home, he could have overcome Rome.

Cornelius Nepos[1]

O ne of the greatest joys in studying the past is to imagine what would have happened if events had turned out differently. It's a popular and understandable opinion among some modern scholars that history results solely from economic and cultural forces far beyond the impact of any one person, but I disagree. Of course, history is shaped by enormous currents that sweep all of us along, but I believe, as do many, that there are certain individuals at certain moments in time that can change everything with a single decision.

Imagine what would have happened if after his overwhelming victory at the Battle of Cannae in the summer of 216 B.C.E., Hannibal had decided to march on Rome and take the city. Could he have succeeded? The question has been a matter of debate for over two thousand years, ever since his lieutenant Maharbal urged Hannibal to strike Rome immediately after that battle. Many Carthaginians at the time believed he could have taken the city, as did many Romans both then and for centuries to come. Hannibal's hesitation was not because of fear or because he thought the sack of Rome was impossible, but because he believed it was unnecessary. By all conventional rules of war, the Romans should have surrendered after losing tens of thousands of men in battle after battle against the Carthaginians. But, as Hannibal learned, the Romans did not play by the same rules as everyone else. They never gave up and they never surrendered.

If Hannibal had realized this after Cannae, he could have and probably would have gathered the eager and numerous armies of Italy to take the city. It would have been a brutal, lengthy campaign of siege, starvation, and assault against a people behind strong, high walls. But in the end, if all of Italy had joined with Hannibal to destroy Rome, the city would have fallen. Hannibal's soldiers and allies would have breached the walls and stormed through the city, raging through the town in a slaughter that would have been fought by Romans resisting until their last breath. But at last, Hannibal would have stood atop the Capitoline Hill in the center of Rome and offered sacrifice to the gods of Carthage for granting him victory. Any surviving Romans would have been sold in the slave markets of the Mediterranean and the treasures of Rome would have been divided among the victors. Hannibal would have sailed home to Carthage in triumph and left the ruins of Rome for the nations of Italy to squabble over. Rome would have come to a bloody end.

But what would that have meant for our history? If there were no Julius Caesar or Augustus, no Hadrian or Constantine—no Roman Empire at all—would the world we live in be different? Of course all we can do is speculate, but I believe we can make some intelligent guesses about how events might have unfolded without Rome.

If Hannibal had destroyed Rome, Italy would have reverted to a land of many independent tribes, cities, and nations all vying for wealth and control in their own part of the peninsula. One of the nearby Etruscan cities would probably have absorbed the seven ruined hills of Rome into their territory. The site of the city itself, with its broken walls and empty Forum filled with grazing sheep, might have become a tourist site for visitors with an interest in the fate of empires. They would have seen a few native inscriptions on stone that survived the sack of the town, but the Latin language would have passed away as a spoken tongue when the last enslaved Romans died—and thus we would have no Spanish, French, or other Romance languages, along with a very different form of English.

The rest of Italy would have prospered without Rome imposing their harsh rule, military conscriptions, and heavy taxes. The Greek cities of the south would have flourished in renewed trade with Carthage, Spain, and the eastern Mediterranean. The mountain tribes in the center of the country would have continued their traditional lives of farming and moving their flocks to summer and winter pastures with the passing seasons. The Celts of the north might have launched occasional raids on their southern neighbors, but in typical Celtic fashion would probably have vented most of their warrior spirit on each other. No Italian city or nation would likely have been able to gain control over the whole peninsula.

In the wider Mediterranean, the Hellenistic revolution begun by Alexander the Great would have continued even without Rome. Greek art, language, literature, philosophy, and culture would have formed a unifying bond between people from Egypt to Spain, though local cultures and languages would have continued to prosper as well. Greek kingdoms such as the Seleucid Empire of Antiochus or the Ptolemaic Kingdom of Egypt would have taken advantage of the vacuum left by Rome and may have found temporary success, but with so many rulers fighting for control it is unlikely that any would gain dominance for long. The Jews of Palestine would still have had their Maccabean revolution against Hellenism, but without the legions of Rome to crush later rebellions, they might have become a major independent political and military force in the eastern Mediterranean for centuries. To the east, the Persians without their Roman adversaries would have had a freer rein to expand their empire and might have put considerable pressure on the Hellenistic and Jewish kingdoms, but probably would not have been able to expand their power permanently to the Mediterranean coast.

And what of Carthage? If Hannibal had destroyed Rome, the Barca family could have become a major force in the Carthaginian state for generations. But the other wealthy families of the city would not have allowed a Barca emperor to rule over them. Spain would have continued to be the prime source of the city's growing wealth, though imperialism on a grander scale was never a Carthaginian goal. The city was a nation of merchants and sailors, not conquerors. Carthage would certainly have become a beacon of civilization in the Mediterranean, perhaps even surpassing Alexandria in Egypt. Its magnificent temples would have overflowed with offerings and its libraries would have amazed visitors who could have read works of literature, science, and religion imported into the city from many lands. Carthage would have become the cosmopolitan center of the Mediterranean and beyond.

Since Carthage was by nature a merchant power, without Roman interference it would have been able to expand its reach to include much of the ancient world. Carthaginian trading posts established along the Atlantic coast of northwest Africa in earlier centuries would have just been the beginning. The merchants of the city would have continued to send colonizing ships down the African coast to the Senegal and Niger River deltas, then on to the southernmost cape of the continent and up the eastern coast to link with trade routes south from Egypt and Persia. The opening of the Mediterranean world to direct trade with eastern Asia would have occurred centuries before the Portuguese and Dutch expeditions we remember today. It's not hard to imagine Carthaginian merchant colonies scattered along the coasts of India, China, and Japan within a few centuries of Hannibal's destruction of Rome. Carthage would have continued its earlier interest in northern Europe as well and established trading posts along the shore of Atlantic Gaul, in Britain and Ireland, and throughout the amber-rich Baltic coast. They could also have sailed west across the Atlantic centuries before Columbus to the vast shores of the Americas to establish lasting and peaceful trade with the Mayans and other

New World peoples, even voyaging around the southern cape to the Pacific coast of both continents. It isn't hard to imagine, just a few centuries after the sack of Rome, two Carthaginian ships meeting at a trading post on the northwest coast of America, one having sailed east from Asia and the other west from Europe, to complete the circumnavigation of the globe. At the very least, Old World agriculture and diet would have been radically altered with the early introduction of previously unknown foods such as potatoes, corn, tomatoes, and chocolate.

A world without Rome would not have been idyllic by any means. Slavery would have been as prevalent and cruel as it was under Rome. There would still have been endless wars fought throughout the world and always the oppression of the weak by the strong. There is also a powerful argument to be made that Rome, however overbearing it could be, provided order to the Mediterranean and Europe that lasted for centuries and allowed civilization to flourish under the emperors. Without the Roman legions, Germanic tribes might have repeatedly overrun southern Europe and plunged the lands of the Mediterranean into chaos. Without Rome, there would also have been no common heritage of law to form the foundation of later European and American governments. And without Rome, Christianity as we know it might have been quite different. With no Pontius Pilate to crucify Jesus, would the new religion have been born? On the other hand, perhaps the message of Christianity would have spread even more widely via Carthaginian trade networks than it did under Roman oppression. Judaism itself may have also prospered without Rome and become a dominant religion in the ancient world. Islam as well, with its roots in Jewish and Christian teachings, may have had a very different history without Rome.

In the end, it isn't really possible to know how the world would have changed if Hannibal had decided to destroy Rome after his victory at Cannae. History is made up of so many complex currents that flow across the centuries. But it is safe to say that a world in which Carthage had won the war against Rome would have been very different from the one we know today.

ANCIENT SOURCES

L ike Socrates and Alexander the Great, Hannibal wrote nothing that has survived the centuries. Thus we rely largely on the testimony of ancient historians for our information on his life, though archaeology and inscriptions can also provide many useful insights. Unfortunately, almost all the written sources on Hannibal were Roman or pro-Roman, though some of them drew on ancient Carthaginian writings, including the lost records of Hannibal's Spartan tutor Sosylos, who accompanied him on his campaign in Italy and composed a seven-volume account of the war.

The most important authors on Hannibal—Polybius and Livy—are available in many fine translations including the bilingual Greek/English and Latin/English editions of the Loeb Classical Library.

Polybius (c. 200–118 B.C.E.) Polybius is our best and most detailed source for the life of Hannibal and the wars of Rome against Carthage. A Greek from the city of Megalopolis in the Peloponnese, Polybius was taken as a young man to Italy as a political hostage and there became friendly with Scipio Aemilianus. He later accompanied Scipio to Spain before retracing Hannibal's route through the Alps and was with Scipio for the destruction of Carthage in 146 B.C.E. Polybius can be overtly pro-Roman in his writing, but he is generally a balanced and reliable guide. As a pragmatic historian, he made careful use of earlier written sources, as well as his own observations on the ground. In his goal of explaining to the Greeks how Rome rose to such great power in the Mediterranean world, his *Histories* covered the period from the beginnings of the First Punic War to the fall of Carthage. Only the first five books of his forty-volume work still survive intact, but ancient and Byzantine writers provide extended excerpts and information from his later books.

Cornelius Nepos (c. 110–24 B.C.E.) Early Roman biographer and friend of Cicero, Nepos composed moralistic and laudatory biographies, including a short life of Hannibal, in his surviving book *On Eminent Foreign Leaders*. It remains the only surviving biography of Hannibal from the ancient world. Nepos was familiar with many earlier sources but could be careless in his use of evidence.

Diodorus of Sicily (first century B.C.E.) Greek historian who wrote a forty-book history of the Mediterranean world from mythological times to 60 B.C.E. Much of his work is lost, but he is an important and often reliable source for the conflict between Rome and Carthage in Sicily before the Punic Wars.

Livy (59–17 C.E.) Roman historian from Patavium (Padua) in northeastern Italy, he composed a history of Rome in 142 books from its foundations as a city (*ab urbe condita*) until the age of Augustus at the beginning of the first century C.E. Books 1–10 (down to 293 B.C.E.) survive, as do Books 21–45 covering the Second Punic War and its aftermath. Livy was a moralizing writer who wished above all to inspire Romans to rise again to greatness by imitating the virtues of their ancestors. He was also much more of a literary historian than the hands-on Polybius, whom he uses extensively, but his account of Hannibal is nonetheless quite valuable, though it must always be read with care because of his deep anti-Carthaginian bias.

Strabo (late first century B.C.E.–early first century C.E.) A Greek geographer and historian from the time of Augustus who included brief sections on Hannibal and Carthage in his work.

Valerius Maximus (early first century C.E.) A minor writer from the age of Tiberius in the first centurty C.E. who passes down some useful information on Hannibal from earlier sources.

Plutarch (c. 50–120 C.E.) The greatest of the classical biographers, Plutarch was a Greek who wrote some of our best and most widely read works on the lives of leading Greeks and Romans. Although he didn't write a biography of Hannibal, he did explore the lives of those, such as Fabius Maximus, who had a direct bearing on his life. Plutarch is a careful writer and usually a sound source for matters touching on Hannibal and Carthage.

Frontinus (first century C.E.) A plainspoken Roman military commander who wrote a handbook called *Strategies* in which he discusses past military leaders, including Hannibal.

Appian (second century C.E.) A Greek historian from Alexandria, he moved to Rome and wrote, like Polybius, an admiring history of Rome for Greek readers. He is best known for his study of the Roman civil wars of the first century B.C.E., but an earlier book of his history is devoted to Rome's conflict with Hannibal. Appian's choice of sources is generally careful and his account of the war with Hannibal can be useful.

Polyaenus (second century C.E.) Macedonian author of eight books on military strategy, a few of which deal with Hannibal's successful battles.

Cassius Dio (c. 164–229 C.E.) Roman senator and historian who served as proconsul of Africa, he wrote an eighty-book history of Rome which makes an attempt to be fair to Rome's enemies, including Hannibal.

Justin (second to fourth century C.E.) Late Roman author who preserves in part the lost *Philippic Histories* of Pomponius Trogus (first century B.C.E.) who wrote on the early history of Carthage.

Ammianus Marcellinus (c. 330–395 C.E.) A Roman military leader and the last of the great Roman historians, he preserves some useful information from earlier writers on Hannibal.

MODERN SOURCES

The last few years have seen a great deal of excellent work illuminating the life of Hannibal and the world in which he lived. A recent rise in research on the Carthaginians has been particularly welcome given that for so long the subject has been largely ignored by classical historians in favor of the Romans.

The best and most readable general history of Hannibal's city is *Carthage Must Be Destroyed: The Rise and Fall of an Ancient Civilization* by Richard Miles. Also important is *The Carthaginians* by Dexter Hoyos, along with *In Search of The Phoenicians* by Josephine Quinn. The older but still very useful *Carthage: A History* by Serge Lancel is well worth any reader's time, particularly for aspects of material culture. Finally, a recent collection of essays by many top scholars on Carthaginian and Punic life is *The Oxford Handbook of the Phoenician and Punic Mediterranean* edited by Carolina López-Ruiz and Brian R. Doak, with up-to-date studies of subjects from Phoenician exploration and Carthaginian Spain to Punic religion and infant sacrifice.

On the Roman side of the Mediterranean, I can think of no better introduction to the rise and fall of Hannibal's implacable foe than the wonderfully readable *SPQR: A History of Ancient Rome* by Cambridge University's Mary Beard. The Second Punic War is most engagingly described for readers in *The Ghosts of Cannae: Hannibal and the Darkest Hour of the Roman Republic* by Robert L. O'Connell. The life of the Carthaginian leader is discussed admirably by Eve MacDonald in her *Hannibal: The Life and Legend* and by Patrick N. Hunt in his *Hannibal*, the latter is particularly useful regarding the route of his march through the Alps. The writing on the Roman and Carthaginian armies by Adrian Goldsworthy in several works, especially his *Cannae: Hannibal's Greatest Victory* and *The Punic Wars*, is essential reading for military history enthusiasts. I must also recommend *Masters of Command: Alexander, Hannibal, Caesar, and the Genius of Leadership* by Barry Strauss for modern lessons from the three greatest generals of the ancient world.

Aubet, Maria Eugenia. *The Phoenicians and the West: Politics, Colonies, and Trade*. Cambridge: Cambridge University Press, 2001.

Badischen Landesmuseum Karlsruhe. *Hannibal ad portas: Macht und Reichtum Karthagos*. Theiss: Stuttgart, 2004.

Beard, Mary. *SPQR: A History of Ancient Rome*. New York: WW Norton, 2015.

Cunliffe, Barry. *The Ancient Celts*. New York: Penguin, 1997.

Fantar, M'hamed Hassine. *Carthage: La cité punique*. Paris: Éditions CNRS, 1995.

Freeman, Philip. *Alexander the Great*. New York: Simon & Schuster, 2011.

Fronda, Michael P. *Between Rome and Carthage: Southern Italy during the Second Punic War*. Cambridge: Cambridge University Press, 2014.

Gabriel, Richard A. *Hannibal: The Military Biography of Rome's Greatest Enemy*. Lincoln, Nebraska: Potomac Books, 2011.

Goldsworthy, Adrian. *The Punic Wars*. London: Cassell, 2000.

———. *The Complete Roman Army*. London: Thames and Hudson, 2003.

———. *Cannae: Hannibal's Greatest Victory*. New York: Basic Books, 2019.

Hoyos, Dexter. *The Carthaginians*. New York: Routledge, 2010.

———. ed. *A Companion to the Punic Wars*. Malden, Massachusetts: Wiley/Blackwell, 2015.

———. *Carthage's Other Wars: Carthaginian Warfare Outside the "Punic Wars" against Rome*. Yorkshire: Pen & Sword Books, 2019.

Hunt, Patrick N. *Hannibal*. New York: Simon & Schuster, 2017.

Lancel, Serge. *Carthage: A History*. Oxford: Blackwell, 1995.

López-Ruiz, Carolina. "Phoenician Literature." In *The Oxford Handbook of the Phoenician and Punic Mediterranean*, edited by Carolina López-Ruiz and Brian R. Doak, 257–269. Oxford: Oxford University Press, 2019.

López-Ruiz, Carolina, and Doak, Brian R., eds. *The Oxford Handbook of the Phoenician and Punic Mediterranean*. Oxford: Oxford University Press, 2019.

MacDonald, Eve. *Hannibal: The Life and Legend*. New Haven: Yale University Press, 2015.

McCarty, Matthew M. "The Tophet and Infant Sacrifice." In *The Oxford Handbook of the Phoenician and Punic Mediterranean*, edited by Carolina López-Ruiz and Brian R. Doak, 311–325. Oxford: Oxford University Press, 2019.

Miles, Richard. *Carthage Must Be Destroyed: The Rise and Fall of an Ancient Civilization*. New York: Penguin, 2010.

O'Connell, Robert L. *The Ghosts of Cannae*. New York: Random House, 2011.

Quinn, Josephine Crawley. *In Search of the Phoenicians*. Princeton: Princeton University Press, 2018.

Scullard, H. H. *Scipio Africanus: Soldier and Politician.* Ithaca: Cornell University Press, 1970.

Strauss, Barry. *Masters of Command: Alexander, Hannibal, Caesar, and the Genius of Leadership.* New York: Simon & Schuster, 2012.

Endnotes

1: Carthage

1   The story of Hannibal's vow, whether true or not, is told best by Polybius (3.11) who reports that Hannibal himself shared the tale in his later years in exile with Antiochus of Syria to convince the king of his undying enmity to Rome and to persuade him to go to war against their common enemy. Livy repeats the story twice with minor variants (21.1, 35.19).

2: Sicily

1   The most detailed version of the foundation of Carthage is found in Justin, *Epitome*, 18.4.

2   For a comprehensive and up-to-date introduction to the Phoenicians, see Quinn, *In Search of the Phoenicians*.

3   Isaiah 23:8.

4   The early history of Carthage is discussed in detail in Lancel, *Carthage*, 1–109; Miles, *Carthage Must Be Destroyed*, 58–95; Hoyos, *The Carthaginians*, 6–58.

5   Only a few details of Himilco's voyage survive in a short, fourth century C.E. work called the *Ora Maritima* by the Roman writer Rufius Festus Avienus, with a brief mention earlier by Pliny (*Natural History*, 2.169). The expedition of Himilco was recorded in a Greek book called the *Periplus*, claiming to be a faithful record of the original inscription from the Temple of Ba'al Hammon in Carthage.

6   Polybius (3.22–23) discovered the text of this treaty in Rome and gives a summary of it, noting that the archaic Latin made it very difficult to read. It defines spheres of trade and pledges that the Carthaginians would build no settlements in Roman territory.

7   Aristotle, *Politics*, 2.1272b.
8   Few other topics in Carthaginian studies are so contested as whether the sacrifices actually occurred and, if so, how often and under what circumstances. Excellent scholars interpret the limited evidence in very different ways. See Lancel, *Carthage*, 193–256; Miles, *Carthage Must Be Destroyed*, 68–73; Hoyos, *The Carthaginians*, 100–105; McCarty, "The Tophet and Infant Sacrifice."
9   Cassius Dio, 43.24.

3: Spain

1   For the military conflicts in period before the Punic Wars, see Hoyos, *The Carthaginians*.
2   Diodorus, 14.41–75.
3   Diodorus, 20.14.
4   The best ancient description of the First Punic War is from Polybius (1.20–63). For modern studies, I recommend Goldsworthy, *The Punic Wars*, 65–140 and the essays in Hoyos, *The Carthaginians*, 129–222.

4: New Carthage

1   Polybius, 1.88, 3.10.
2   The Roman historian Cornelius Nepos (*Hamilcar*, 4) says that "with horses, weapons, men, and money, he enriched all of Africa."

5: Saguntum

1   Valerius Maximus, 9.3.
2   Cornelius Nepos, *Hannibal*, 13.2.
3   Thucydides, *Peloponnesian War*, 2.45.2.
4   Livy, 24.41.7; Silius Italicus, *Punica*, 3.97,106.
5   Livy, 21.4.
6   3.15.
7   Polybius, 2.13.
8   Polybius, 2.36.
9   Livy, 21.3. As always in ancient speeches, we should be suspicious that the reported speaker said these words, but the sentiment seems accurate.

6: Gaul

1   Polybius, 3.13; Livy, 21.5.

2   Polybius, 3.13.6.
3   Polybius, 3.14; Livy, 21.5.
4   Polybius (3.17) has surprisingly little to say about the attack on Saguntum, so our main source is Livy (21.7–16) who turns the siege into a drama (or melodrama) comparable to the Greek assault on Troy. Silius Italicus presents an even more romanticized account in his epic *Punica* (1–2).
5   Zonaras, 8.22.2–3. Compare Livy, 21.16 and Polybius, 3.20.
6   Polybius, 3.33.1–4.

7: The Alps
1   Polybius, 3.35.
2   Livy, 21.23.1.
3   Polybius, 3.40.

8: The Ticinus River
1   Polybius, 3.49.5; Livy, 21.31.4.
2   The best modern description of Hannibal's possible route over the Alps is Hunt (2017).
3   Polybius, 9.24.4–8.
4   Polybius, 3.54.
5   Livy, 21.37.
6   Polybius, 3.60.7-8.
7   Polybius, 3.56.4; Livy, 21.38.5.

9: Trebia
1   Polybius, 3.63.4.
2   Polybius, 3.64–66; Livy, 21.45–46. Livy admits it may have in fact been a Ligurian slave instead of the younger Scipio who saved his father.
3   Polybius, 3.66–67.
4   Polybius, 3.69; Livy, 21.48.

10: The Arno Marshes
1   Polybius, 3.68-70; Livy, 21.49–51.
2   Polybius, 3.71–74; Livy, 21.54–57.

11: Lake Trasimene
1   Livy, 21.62.
2   Polybius, 3.78.1–4.
3   Polybius, 3.78–79; Livy, 22.2.

12: Campania
1   Polybius, 3.82–84; Livy, 22.5–7.
2   Polybius, 3.86; Livy, 22.8.

13: Geronium
1   *Thesaurus Linguae Etruscae*, 890.
2   Polybius, 3.87–88.
3   Polybius, 3.90–91.
4   Livy, 22.14.3.
5   Polybius, 3.93–94; Livy, 22.16.
6   Polybius, 3.97.

14: Cannae
1   Polybius, 3.100; Livy, 22.18.
2   Polybius, 3.101.
3   Polybius, 3.103; Plutarch, *Fabius*, 8.
4   Livy, 22.33.

15: Rome
1   Polybius, 3.110.
2   Polybius, 3.111.
3   Polybius, 3.112–116; Livy, 22.46.
4   Livy, 22.49-51; Polybius, 3.117.

16: Capua
1   Livy, 22.51.1–4.
2   Livy, 22.58.
3   Livy, 22.57.2–3.
4   Livy, 22.59–61.

17: Metaurus
1   Livy, 23.11–13.
2   Livy, 23.1–8.
3   Livy, 23.14–16.
4   Livy, 24.34.
5   Polybius, 9.5–6; Livy, 26.7–11.

18: Zama
1   Livy, 26.18.
2   Polybius, 10.7–15; Livy, 26.19–47.

3   Livy, 27.15.
4   Livy, 27.36–51; Polybius, 11.1.
5   Polybius, 11.20–24; Livy, 28.12–15.

19: Exile
1   Livy, 29.30–33.
2   Livy, 29.6–10.
3   Livy, 30.6.
4   Livy, 30.12–15.
5   Polybius, 15.5–8; Livy, 30.30.
6   Polybius, 15.9–15.

20: Legacy
1   Polybius, 15.18; Livy, 30.37.
2   Cornelius Nepos, *Hannibal*, 7.5.
1   Valerius Maximus, 5.3.2b.

Ancient Sources
1   Cornelius Nepos, *Hannibal*, 1.

INDEX

A

Aemilius Paulus, Lucius, 122–123, 128–130, 132, 133
Aeneid (Virgil), 2
Aeolian Islands, 15
Agathocles, 13
Akra Leuke, 29–30
Alexander the Great, xii, 12–13, 19, 56–57, 93, 182, 192
Allobroges tribe, 60–62
Alps, 52–54, 58, 59–66
Althea, 39–40
ancient sources, 197–200
Antiochus III, 179–181, 183
Apennine Mountains, 89, 90–91
Apollo, 139
Appian, 199–200
Apulia, 108–109, 113–114, 117–123, 126
Archimedes, 148
Aristotle, 6
Arno marshes, 87–94
Astapa, 163
Athens, 1, 6, 20

B

Ba'al Hammon, x, 8, 9, 13
Babylon, 13
Baecula, 160
Balearic Islands, 51, 116
Barca family, x, 18, 26, 34, 35, 44, 50, 108, 116, 142, 153, 192–193.
    See also specific members
battle psychology, 127

Boii tribe, 50, 71, 89
Bruttium, 163–164
Byblos, 2
Byrsa, 2

C

Cacus, 52
Cadiz, 3
Caesar, Julius, xii, 9, 53
Campania, 105–116, 145–147, 150
Cannae, 125–133, 156, 190
cannibalism, 63
Capua, 141–151, 158
Carpetani tribe, 40–41, 54
Cartala, 39–40
Carthage, ix–xi, 1–9; Alexander the Great and, 13; allies of, 72, 141–142, 145–147, 153–154, 159, 164; attacks on, 11–14, 16; conquest of Spain by, 21–30; control of Spain by, 27–34, 153–154, 159–160; defeat of, 170–171, 175, 178–179; defense of, 7; destruction of, 138, 186; economy of, 4; exploration by, 5–6; fate of, without Rome, 192–194; founding of, 1–2; Hannibal's return to, 172–176; interests of, 153–154; invasion of, by Rome, 166–171; libraries of, 19–20; life in, 7–8, 20; location of, 3–4; Mago's return to, 142–144; messages to, 108; peace negotiations with Rome by, 170–171, 178–179; political system of, 6–7; religion

in, 8–9; riches of, 177–178; Roman threat to, 165–166; Rome and, x, xi, 6, 14–17, 23–24, 36, 43–44, 46–47, 49–50, 67–77; senate of, 7; Syracuse and, 11–14; as trading center, 4–6

Carthaginian army: allies of, 60, 68–69, 75, 76–77, 80–82, 89–90, 93–94; in Apulia, 108–109; attacks on, by local tribes, 61–63; in Campania, 110–116; at Cannae, 125–133; casualties in, 64, 66, 101; crossing of Alps by, 59–66; fight against Rome by, 51–58; in Geronium, 117–123; Hannibal as general of, 36, 39–47, 49–58, 83, 107–108; at Lake Trasimene, 98–101; local inhabitants of Italy and, 68–70, 76–77; march through Arno marshes by, 87–94; military tactics of, 72–74; occupation of Italy by, 141–142, 144–151; in Picenum, 107–108; recruits to, 107, 108, 143–144; resources for, 143–144, 158–159; size of, 97; soldiers in, 51; in Spain, 36, 39–47, 49–58, 154–158; at Ticinus River battle, 71–77; at Trebia, 80–85

Carthalo, 140
Cassius Dio, 200
Cato, Marcus Porcius, 185, 186
Caudex, Appius Claudius, 15
cavalry horses, 108, 118
Celtiberians, 27, 28, 29
Celtic prisoners, treatment of, 69–70, 90
Celts: allies, 72, 75, 80–82, 87–94, 108, 143, 147; Allobroges tribe, 60–62; Boii tribe, 50, 71, 89; hostile, 34, 40–41, 53, 54–55, 60–63, 71; in Italy, 36, 54–56, 68–70, 72, 75, 76, 80–82, 192; soldiers, 31, 51, 72–74, 76, 84, 97, 99–101, 131, 136; in Spain, 24, 27–29, 34, 40, 41; Taurini tribe, 68–69; Volcae tribe, 56

Cerne Island, 5

Christianity, 194
Clastidium, 76
Clitomachus, 20
Corsica, 23, 24, 49
Cyprus, 1, 3

D

Dasius, 76
David (king), 1
Diodorus of Sicily, 198
Dionysius, 12

E

Ebro River, 53
Ebro Treaty, 36, 43, 44, 53
elephants, 14, 29, 31, 52, 54, 56–57, 90, 176
Elissa (queen), 1–2, 3, 4
Emporium, 156
Ephesus, 181–182
Epona, 28
Etruscans, 107
Eumenes, 183
exile, 177–184

F

Fabius Maximus, Quintus, xix, 46, 105–114, 149, 158, 166; as general, 108–114; leadership of, 105–106, 119–120, 121; return to Rome by, 118; Scipio and, 160; strategy of, 109–112, 147–148
Fabius Pictor, 139
First Punic War, 23, 36
Flaccus, Publius Valerius, 42–43
Flaminius, Gaius, xix, 88, 95, 96–101, 103
fortified cities, 136
Frontinus, 199

G

Gades, 3, 25–26, 27, 51
Gadir, 25–26
Gaul, 49–58, 160, 161
Gauls, 22, 50
Gelon, 11
Genoa, 163

Geronium, 117–123
Gibraltar, 25
gods, x, 8, 26, 28, 51–52, 89, 102–103, 139, 149
gold mines, 24, 28–29
government: of Carthage, 6–7; of Rome, 79–80, 105, 127–128
grain, 60, 76, 94, 117, 126, 172
Greece, 3, 192
Greek language, 19, 32

H
Hamilcar Barca, x–xi, xix; death of, 34; Helice campaign of, 33–34; in Sicily, 16–17; in Spain, 24–32
Hannibal, xx; alliance building by, 40–41, 69, 88–90, 107, 141–142, 144–147; assault on Saguntum by, 44–47; attack on Rome by, 149–151, 190–191; in Campania, 110–116; at Cannae, 125–133; care for soldiers by, 40, 83, 107–108, 164; crossing of Alps by, 59–66; death of, 183–184; education of, 19, 32; in exile, 177–184; Fabius and, 108–109; family of, x, 18, 26, 34, 35, 44, 50, 108, 116, 142, 153, 192–193; Flaminius and, 96–101; as general of Carthaginian army, 36, 39–47, 49–58, 83, 107–108; greatness of, xi–xiii; hatred of Rome by, ix–xi, 17, 43, 137; imagined victory by, 189–195; injuries suffered by, 92–93; invasion of Italy by, 58, 67–77; leadership of, 34–35, 122, 127, 164; legacy of, 185–188; in Locri, 167–168; march through Arno marshes by, 87–94; meeting between Scipio and, 174–175, 182; military tactics of, 41, 72–74, 82–83, 130–132; military training of, 31–32; opposition to, 36–37; political career of, 179–180; reputation of, 41–42; retreat from Italy by, 171–172; return to Carthage by, 172–176; scorched-earth policy of, 98, 107;
in Spain, 24–30, 33–35, 39–47; strategy of, 88, 97–100, 111, 113–114, 125–126; successes against Romans by, xii, 55–58, 71–74, 81–85, 97–101, 114, 121–122, 132–133, 135; threat of, 159; at Ticinus River battle, 71–77; tomb of, 188; at Trebia, 79–85; trial of, 179; youth of, 18–20, 31–33; at Zama, 174–176
Hanno (explorer), xx, 5–6, 54
Hanno (lieutenant), 32, 54, 56, 115
Hanno (nobleman), xx, 23–24, 29, 36–37, 44, 47, 50, 108, 143–144
Hasdrubal Barca, xx, 18, 20, 32, 34–36, 51, 115–116, 154–155, 159–162
Hasdrubal Gisgo, 157, 163, 167, 168, 169
Helice, 33–34
Hellenism, 192
Heracles, 25, 26
Hercules, 26, 29, 51–52, 89, 149
Hermandica, 40
Herodotus, 5–6
Himera, 11–12
Himilco, 5
Homer, 19
horses, 108, 118
human sacrifice, x, 8–9, 13, 139–140

I
Iberia, 3, 153–154, 156. *See also* Spain
Iberian tribes, 27–29
Ilipa, Battle of, 165
Illurgia, 163
Illyria, 36, 43, 44, 46, 123
Imilce, 33
infanticide, 9
Insubres tribe, 69
Isaiah, 3
Islam, 194
Italy, 4, 6; anti-Rome sentiment in, 67–68, 76–77, 90, 110–111, 145; Carthaginian occupation of,

141–142, 144–151; invasion of, by
Hannibal, 58, 67–77

J
Jerusalem, 1
Jesus Christ, 194
Jews, 192
Judaism, 194
Junius, Marcus, 140
Justin, 200

K
Kerkennah, 181

L
Laelius, Gaius, 156, 166, 169
Lake Trasimene, 95–103
Latin language, 191
lectisternium, 102–103
Leonidas, 19
libraries, 19–20
Lilybaeum, 14
Livius Salinator, Marcus, 161–162
Livy, xiii, 39, 59, 65, 89, 118, 171,
188, 198–199
Locri, 167–168
Lugus, 28

M
Maccabean revolution, 192
Macedonia, 6, 147
Magilus, 58
Mago (author), 19
Mago (brother), xx, 18, 32; death of,
171; in Italy, 159–160, 163, 166;
return to Carthage by, 142–144;
in Spain, 154, 162–163; at Trebia,
82, 84, 91
Mago (naval commander), 14
Magonids, 11–12
Mago the Samnite, 32
Maharbal, xx, 45, 102, 135, 190
Marcellinus, Ammianus, 200
Marcellus, Marcus Claudius,
146–147, 160–161
Masinissa (prince), xx, 154, 165–167,
169–170, 178

Massalia, 53, 54, 55
Mauritania, 5
Maximus, Valerius, 186, 199
Melqart, 8, 26, 29, 51–52
mercenary soldiers, 7, 12, 17, 26, 29
Messana, 15
Metaurus, 153–164
Middle Ages, 188
military tactics, 41; of Carthaginian
army, 72–74; of Hannibal, 82–83,
130–132; of Roman army, 72,
129–130, 156–157
Minucius Rufus, Marcus, 106, 109,
111–112, 114, 118–121, 133
modern sources, 201–204
molk, x, 8–9
Motya, 12

N
Naples, 145
Napoleon, 66, 188
naval warfare, 16
navy, 15, 17, 25
Nebuchadnezzar (king), 5
Nepos, Cornelius, 189, 198
Nero, Gaius Claudius, 161–162
New Carthage, 31–37, 39, 40, 51, 52,
157–158, 163
Nola, 146–147
Numidia, 18, 25, 165–167
Numidian cavalry, 57–58, 73–74,
83–84, 91, 100, 102, 128, 144,
161, 174

O
Oestrymnians, 5
Olcades tribe, 39
omens, 88–89, 103

P
pack animals, 62–64, 65, 91, 92, 94
Palestine, 192
peace negotiations, x, 12, 17, 137,
138, 170–171, 178–179
Peloponnesian War, 148
Pericles, 33
Persian Empire, 12–13, 56–57, 192

phalarica, 45
Philip V, 147
Phoenicians, 2–3, 5–6
pillaging, 94
Pillars of Hercules, 3, 5
Placentia, 75–76, 85
Plato, 20
Plutarch, 199
Polyaenus, 200
Polybius, xx, 23, 41–42, 59–60, 63, 64, 66, 96, 171, 197–198
Pontius Pilate, 194
Po River, 64, 68, 75, 81, 87, 96, 161
prisoners of war, 69–70, 90, 100–102, 138–139
Prusias, 183
psychological warfare, 69, 75, 127, 149, 174
Ptolemaic Kingdom, 192
Pulcher, Claudius, 16
Punic alphabet, 3
Punic colonies, x
Punic language, 19–20
Pygmalion, 1
Pyrenees Mountains, 53–54
Pyrrhic victory, 14
Pyrrhus, xx, 13–14, 138, 182

Q
Quinctius Crispinus, Titus, 161

R
Regulus, 16
religion, 194; Carthagianian, 8–9; Roman, 88–89, 102–103
Remus, 1
Rhône River, 56, 57
ritual combat, 70
Roman army, 50, 52; at Cannae, 125–133; casualties in, 100–101, 132–133; defeats of, xii, 55–58, 71–74, 81–85, 87–88, 97–101, 114, 121–122, 132–133, 135; under Fabius, 105–114; under Flaminius, 96–101; invasion of Carthage by, 166–171; at Lake Trasimene, 98–101; leadership of, 127–128;

military tactics of, 72, 129–130, 156–157; new recruits to, 95–96, 106–107, 123, 140; under Scipio, 69, 71–77; under Sempronius, 79–85; under Servilius, 101–102; size of, 123, 126–127; in Spain, 154–158, 163; at Ticinus River battle, 71–77; at Trebia, 79–85; victories by, 158–159, 160, 162, 163
Roman Empire, 187–188, 191
Roman navy, 15, 16, 50
Roman prisoners, 90, 100–102, 138–139
Roman Republic, 21–22; political system of, 127–128; system of government in, 79–80, 105
Roman warfare, 22, 138, 142
Rome: attack on, 149–151, 190–191; Carthage and, x, xi, 6, 14–17, 23–24, 36, 43–44, 46–47, 49–50, 67–77; conquests by, 16, 22–23; end of war with, 137–138; expansion by, 13, 187; founding of, 1, 6; history without, 189–195; impact of Hannibal on, 186–187; New Carthage and, 36; peace negotiations with, 138–139, 140, 142, 178–179; reaction of, to Hannibal's victories, 87–89, 102–103, 121–122, 139–140, 161; reasons not to attack, 135–137; Saguntum and, 42–47; wars fought by, 21–22
Romulus, 1

S
sacrifice: of children, 13; of firstborn, x, 8–9; by Romans, 9, 139–140
Saguntum, 39–47, 50, 51, 136
Salamanca, 40
Sardinia, 3, 4, 23, 24, 49, 95, 147
Scipio, Aemilianus, 186
Scipio, Gnaeus, 95, 114–116, 154, 155
Scipio, Publius Cornelius, 21, 50, 53, 55, 58, 67, 69, 71–77, 80, 81, 85, 114, 154

Scipio Africanus, Publius Cornelius, xx; at Cannae, 133, 156; in Carthage, 172–176; death of, 186; as general, 155–158, 160, 163, 166–176; invasion of Africa by, 166–171; in Locri, 167–168; meeting between Hannibal and, 174–175, 182; respect for Hannibal by, 179, 180; retirement of, 185–186; at Trebia, 85
scorched-earth policy, 98, 107
Seleucid Empire, 192
Sempronius Gracchus, Tiberius, 140
Sempronius Longus, Tiberius, 50, 67, 79–85; defeat of, at Trebia, 84–85, 87–88
Servilius Geminus, Gnaeus, 88, 95–96, 101–102
Severans, 187
Severus, Septimius, 187–188
Sibylline Books, 139
Sicily, x, 4, 11–20, 23, 24, 49, 50, 95, 148, 165
Sidon, 2
sieges, of fortified cities, 136
silver coins, 29
silver mines, 3, 24, 26, 28–29
slavery, 8, 194
Sophonisba, 167, 169–170
Sosylos, 19, 32
Spain, 3, 4, 21–30; battles in, 154–158, 162–163; Carthaginian army in, 36, 39–47, 49–58, 154–158; Carthaginian control of, 27–34, 153–154, 159–160; Celts in, 24, 27–29, 34, 40, 41; Hamilcar's campaign in, 24–32; Hannibal in, 24–30, 33–35, 39–47; loss of, by Carthage, 49–50; New Carthage, 31–37, 39, 40, 51, 52, 157–158, 163; Romans in, 114–116, 154–158, 163, 165
Strabo, 199
suffetes, 7
Syphax (king), 166–167, 168, 169
Syracuse, 11–15, 147, 148, 158

T
Tamphilus, Quintus Baebius, 42–43
Tanit, 8
Tarentum, 13, 95, 147, 158–159
Tartessus, 3, 26
Taurini tribe, 68–69
Terillus, 11
Theseus, 1
Ticinus River, 67–77, 155–156
timeline, xv–xvii
total war, 137
trade, 3–6, 42, 54, 56, 180, 191, 193–194
Trebia, 79–85, 163
Troy, 136
Tyre, x, 1–5, 13, 181

U
Utica, 168, 169

V
Vaccaei tribe, 40–41
Varro, Gaius Terentius, xix, 122–123, 128–133, 156
Vestal Virgins, 139
Virgil, 2
Volcae tribe, 56
Vulso, Lucius Manlius, 50, 71

W
warfare, 22; naval, 16; psychological, 69, 75, 127, 149, 174; Roman, 22, 138, 142; siege, 136
women: in ancient world, 33; in Carthage, 7; in Hannibal's life, 32–33; slaves, 8

Z
Zama, 174–176
Zonaras, 46